UNLEASH THE PSYCHIC IN YOU

UNLEASH THE PSYCHIC IN YOU

How To Trust Your Intuition for Successful Decision Making

trust it
press

To receive Joanna's free weekly newsletter
Confessions of a Psychic and tune into her TV show
visit **www.AmericasIntuitionCoach.com**.

For quantity discounts, promotions, or sponsorship of *Unleash the Psychic in You*, please call
1-877-822-5142 (toll free).

ISBN Number: 978-0-9820808-0-1

Printed in the United States of America.

To my husband Nick, the love of my life

TABLE OF CONTENTS

I'm Not Your Typical Psychic

I'm Over Psychic Sensationalism

Clarity Leads to More Satisfying Relationships

Your Intuition Will Show You the Way

Deep Healing

The Other Side

Rock Bottom

Lights, Camera, Action

Destructive Expectations

Bright Shiny Psychic Syndrome

A Different Paradigm

Your Intuition Is Never Wrong

Commit to Your Intuition Development

Go with Your Intuitive Flow

Intuition with Benefits

Your Six Senses

Intuition Development Meditation Techniques

ACKNOWLEDGMENTS

This book is a milestone of achievement and healing for my soul. There is no way I could have written *Unleash the Psychic in You* without the constant, steady support of my husband Nick Garzilli. His belief in me and his love have fueled my passion to be the creative soul I am.

I would also like to extend my heartfelt gratitude to the following individuals:

To my dear friend and soul sister Kim Castle, who moved me through my writer's block. Kim's visionary nature. Courage, and leadership skills were the reason this book happened. Without her wisdom, this book wouldn't be in your hands.

To my publishing consultant Stephanie Gunning, who is a blessing in my life. This book wouldn't be complete without your powerful vision and brilliance.

To my parents and parents-in-law for loving me.

To all of my clients, customers, and newsletter subscribers. You are my inspiration! You make me want to write.

To all of my spiritual mentors and teachers, including those on the Other Side (Grandpa Lou Lou).

To my pets, Winston, Stella, and Courvoisier, who bring me much joy.

Thank you God for your infinite wisdom.

FOREWORD
Kim Castle

In past near two decades I've had the amazing great fortune to guide thousands of people to get in touch with what they were put on this planet to do, to grow that purpose to big heights as a business, and to communicate "it" to the world. Joanna Garzilli is one of those people. From the first moment I met Joanna, I knew she had so much to offer the world—more than she even realized. Although she had already achieved great success and acclaim, she had barely scratched the surface. Her book, *Unleash the Psychic in You*, is simply a glimmer of the universe she offers us all.

To realize that each and every one of us has the ability to be our own psychics, meaning to understand that we all literally have the inborn capability to tap into an unknown greater source of wisdom and perceive our own futures, is at once exciting, scary, and almost unbelievable. This native gift is often hard for us to accept as real. At some level we look at the challenges in our lives and hold them against ourselves, as if they are evidence that we are less than. "If I were so evolved as to be psychic and able to interpret my best future for myself, then why would I be going through the challenges that I am going through?" we ask, doubting the possibility.

Denial of our intuitive gifts happens in the dark places of our minds and hearts, and it often goes so far back that we don't even realize any self-diminishing thoughts are there. We believe we must be broken, so we look to get fixed. It's in this moment that we typically look outside of ourselves for an answer, for help, for guidance from someone who knows. And who better, we imagine, than someone who can "see the future"?

Our pure desire to receive guidance causes us to view professional psychics with their heightened skills as more special and more perfect than us. We gladly put them on a crystal pedestal to do their magic for us. Hungry for insight, we put our faith in them to tell us our destiny, and hand over our personal power in the process. And a vast majority of people who have developed their intuitive skills to a professional level gladly let us.

Fortunately, Joanna is not one of those people. While she's earned the right to stand alongside John Edwards and James Van Praagh with her own wildly successful television show in the UK, Joanna is not your mother's Sylvia Browne. She delivers the goods in a hip and witty manner. Her insights both inspire and sting with truth.

Joanna is a gifted individual who provides a refreshingly honest twist on intuition and the ups and downs of being a psychic. She lays everything, including her personal life, on the line. Without censorship, in *Unleash the Psychic in You* Joanna bares all from the heart: her pain, her darkness, her flaws, and the series of bad decisions she made that took her from the heights of privileged London high society to living in a tiny basement apartment with no heat and no money to her name, as well as the guiding force that led her back to a place of unyielding dignity, love, compassion, and true success.

A saint she's not. She's much more. Joanna is a powerful example of what it means to be an evolving spirit on this planet. She gladly shows us all how to do the same as she did and shows us how to follow in her footsteps. She shares the gifts she came into this life with openly, not because she believes she is more special than the rest of us but because she knows that each and every one of us is special in our own right.

Joanna is a beautiful, honest demonstration of something that each of us can do for ourselves. Not only does she believe this, she reveals the practical steps to develop and trust our innate guidance system, our own intuition, so that we may be our own guiding force in our lives.

You hold in your hands the way there.

Simply suspend all judgment of yourself... Just for the moment, open your heart wide, apply these practical steps, and, in Joanna's words, "Tune in and trust it."

INTRODUCTION

I'm most grateful you have this book in your hands. Why? It is filled with gifts that I hope you will be inspired to apply in your own life.

I have to admit this book started out as a diamond in the rough. It took me several years to get *Unleash the Psychic in You* out of my head and onto the page. It would have happened much faster if my ego had moved aside. I blocked myself from writing because I got caught up in my concerns of what you would think of me and of the things you might say. I was embarrassed to put myself out there and publicly reveal, "I'm a psychic medium."

Until recently, there have been so many negative connotations about psychics and, in some cases, rightly so. Have you ever gone for a psychic reading and come out feeling more deflated and frustrated than before you went in? I know I have on numerous occasions.

I wrote this book because I realized that all of the guidance and support we desire is already inside us. You don't need to go to someone else for the answers. It is my hope, you will learn from my mistakes. I made many of them. I'm going to share with you candidly about my past because I want you to go easy on yourself as you learn to trust your intuition.

All too often psychics are put on a pedestal; they are perceived as gods. I'm not kidding. I remember being hired as a psychic for a Hollywood fashion designer's birthday bash. There were many movers and shakers, swishing around with champagne in hand and dressed from head to toe in luxurious clothing with a capital "L." You may think to yourself, "These people live the life. They are beautiful, successful, and rich." They were . . . until they sat down away from the hustle and bustle of the party. Then their demeanor transformed, their party masks were removed, and their emotional baggage was dumped in front of me like a massive pile of shit. Yes, crap. And they wanted me to clean it up energetically for them in a five- to ten-minute psychic reading. It's not fair to put a psychic on the receiving end of this offload because it is unrealistic for a person about to receive a reading to expect a psychic to transform his or her life in such a short span of time.

As a psychic, you have to command strong boundaries or you'll be drained in a heartbeat. You have to be prepared for anything in a psychic reading, but especially at a party. Where there's a party, there is alcohol. That presents an obstacle to a psychic's ability to get a clear read off someone asking for guidance.

I remember a very well put together woman sitting in front of me who asked me to justify her affair. That is not a psychic's job. I worked at the same party a year later and some of the attendees seemed as if they were stuck in a time warp. They had the same problems and they still wondered why these problems were happening to them. What did all these people have in common? They didn't want to take responsibility for their lives. They wanted me to say, "There, there, everything is all right."

That kind of reassurance doesn't help anyone. When you are out of energetic alignment it doesn't matter what anyone says of does. You will still feel awful because the imbalance lies within you.

This book will help you open up to your own inner guidance and discover that all your answers lie within you. It is my intention for you to experience a deep sense of healing and inner knowing as you gradually open your heart by following the steps laid out in this book. I also want you to know it is safe to unleash the psychic in you. When you remain receptive and let go of trying to force an outcome, intuition flows and the realm of spirit is accessible to you. Spirit will never harm you. I want to show you how you can experience absolute clarity. Trusting yourself is the most amazing feeling. It's liberating and opens up your creativity in a way greater than you can imagine.

I'm Not Your Typical Psychic

I want to share a little about myself so you'll understand how I became America's Intuition Coach™. Several times in the past I resisted my destiny because the responsibility frightened me. I thought, "Who am I to tell people what to do with their lives?" What I learned was that it is my responsibility to guide people to see their own gifts and talents, to see the beauty of their relationships, to understand when it is time to let go of a business or a marriage, or to know when it is time to travel to a different country to start a new life.

When I stopped worrying about what people thought, I found that great strength and clarity flowed into the guidance I gave. I became acutely aware that the opposite of worrying is nurturing, and once I shifted from worrying about what people thought to caring about people and nurturing them, it enabled me to be a pure channel for spirit.

I found myself doing medium readings and would be amazed when someone who had passed over communicated through me from the spirit world. I was surprised as the person who was receiving the reading. I'd go over and over the information in my mind once the client had left. I'd rationalize the experience and try to find a tangible explanation for the intangible. My proof was that my client had shared the same experience and found the information to be accurate.

As a psychic, you'd think I'd have no fear of death. For a long time I was terrified. But my experiences doing medium readings have confirmed to me that our spirits do live on once we die. Knowing the name, age, sex, or cause of a person's death I'd never met is always a very humbling experience for me.

A client of mine once emailed me and said that her church group said, "Psychics cannot be connected to God." That's not true for me. I live my life by God's guidance. It is my will to do God's work. Yes, I love Gucci, Prada, and sex, however that doesn't mean I'm egotistical or disconnected from spirit. You don't have to give up everything you love to connect to your intuition.

At one time I thought that if I was to be pure and spiritual, I had to let go of everything material. I was also afraid that people would say, "She can't be spiritual because she's materialistic." Now I look back and can't believe I gave away my Louis Vuitton handbag that I loved. Since those days I've learned that if a material possession makes you feel good—for instance, if you want a Porsche because you love the purr of the engine and the shape of the chassis—there's nothing wrong with that. You only disconnect from your intuition when you want to use the car to get laid or as a status symbol. Even if you do get what you want in such cases, you won't feel good about it inside if your intentions are not aligned with spirit.

I'm a regular person who happens to be a gifted psychic medium who used to be a London party girl. Yes, I dated some pretty hot celebrities (including Antonio Banderas) before I met my gorgeous husband Nick. We met through my friend Caroline who invited me into her sketch comedy group because she wanted to emulate my British accent for a skit about two old ladies gossiping and commenting on the six thousand dollar feather Camilla Parker Bowles wore for her wedding to Prince Charles.

My life isn't extraordinary or weird. I live in Los Angeles with Nick, our two cats, Stella and Courvoisier, and our dog, Winston (named after Winston Churchill). He's a Cockapoo and so cute. I always dreamed of living in a house with a pool surrounded by palm trees. I'm most grateful that is now my reality. Nick and I love going for a good French breakfast followed by walking Winston on the beach in Malibu. I have wonderful friends and I love my parents very much.

In the past, as I developed my intuition, I had a challenging relationship with my family. I often felt misunderstood and I blamed them. That wasn't cool. They were doing their best. I sometimes isolated myself. But most of the time I'd be super social. I was always going to parties and I had four phones that rang off the hook, but I felt very alone. Being superficial was the way I protected myself from feeling spirit.

Developing my intuition has helped me to understand people better. That understanding opened a door to my healing. It is my honor to share my journey with you.

I'm Over Psychic Sensationalism

Many excellent books on psychic development and intuition are available that are packed full of techniques. So why read *Unleash the Psychic in You*? The biggest thing I've learned that I want to share with you is that being psychic doesn't mean you have no problems and know all the answers. It takes time to develop a strong foundation of intuition. You can read a thousand books on clairvoyance, but if you're in deep pain—pain from your past that possibly you are even unaware of—knowing different techniques and doing exercises will do nothing to help you in your own life.

I am sharing my personal mistakes and successes so you will have a map to guide you on your own path. I want you to know that you can screw up, feel negative, and still be tapped into your intuition. Here's an example. I remember sitting with my dear friend Pam and obsessing over a text message from a guy I was dating. The text said, "Hey." I asked her, "Pam, does this mean, 'Hey, I want to see you later?' or 'Hey, I'm keeping my distance and you on the backburner'?" I was stuck. But ten minutes later, I was able to switch gears to absolute knowing and give a client a crystal clear psychic reading. I could see a probable future for my client that went two years ahead in time. So why couldn't I see the truth for myself? Had my intuition stopped working? No. My intuition was working. I was just blocking it in my own case.

In this book you're going to read about some of my personal agonies so that you'll be able to apply what I learned about how to handle them to situations in your own life. I'm going to give you guidance as to how to take your next best step.

Clarity Leads to More Satisfying Relationships

If you want to experience clarity in your life, this book is for you. If you want to overcome your limiting beliefs, there are many hidden gems of healing in these pages. I began soul searching fifteen years ago. It took me fifteen years to grasp what I'm going to share with you. The great news is that when you do experience clarity it's like a switch is flipped and your light turns on. Once you have this awareness, things don't bother you the way they did in the past. It's easier to forgive people because you can see the truth of their actions even when they can't. You can help others because you have the advantage of responding in a non-reactive way to a person who is unconsciously hurting you. Often when a client has been upset about a relationship, I've helped them see why the other person is behaving in a particular way.

This book will help you deepen your communication with the people you love and the people you work with. Ninety percent of the time if there is a misunderstanding it's because we do not know how we feel ourselves. We are often oblivious to our own thought processes. It is your responsibility to become conscious if you want to live a life filled with love, happiness, and success. When you make the choice to live an intuitive life amazing things will happen.

Don't let your life pass you by. Don't carry remorse, regret, or sadness for the things you didn't do that you dreamed of doing. Don't die without letting someone you care for know how much you love him or her. I see so many people who feel that they have no control over their lives. They are overwhelmed. They think, "I can't do anything about my situation." That's not true. There is guidance available to you 24/7. You have access to knowledge and wisdom that can support you in every step of your life. All you have to do for now is be willing to open yourself up to guidance. There is a spirit guide waiting for you, ready to work with you, and willing to teach you whatever you want to know. Take advantage of this opportunity now.

Your Intuition Will Show You the Way

It is my hope that you develop and cultivate your intuition so you may experience self-confidence that exudes from your aura. People will feel at peace and calm in your presence. They will sense that you have something profound to offer and you don't need to say it. You don't need to prove yourself to anyone. You don't need to justify who you are, what you buy, whom you date, or where you go. It's none of anyone else's business because when you take every step from intuition, every action in your life is taken from a deep sense of clarity, from the guidance of your heart and soul.

Think about how wonderful it would be to be a calm reassuring presence for your family, friends, and loved ones. Imagine what your life could be like with no struggle or resistance. Persistence pays off. If you commit to a path of true self-discovery through the development of your intuition the rewards will exceed your expectations. You'll see when you experience it.

You don't have to be psychic to read this book. You don't even have to know what the word "psychic" means. All you have to do is be willing to be receptive. I suggest you read this book several times or open it on a random page for a pearl of wisdom. Or you can close your eyes, take a deep breath, and let a number pop into your head. Then open the book to this page. Spirit loves communicating messages in this way because it takes the pressure off of you having to be at a certain psychic level.

When I first got into psychic development, I was pretty competitive. I thought if I knew the name of every ascended master, the meanings of every chakra, and all about multi-dimensional realities, I'd be a better psychic. Not the case. When you meet a boastful psychic, it usually means that individual is not a particularly good psychic. I've had housewives and bankers attend my workshops who were far more intuitive than professional psychics.

My understanding of psychic ability in its purest form is that it involves acceptance of self. When you are psychic, you can see the truth. All a psychic does is remove the veils of darkness and illusion. Anyone can do that. You can do that if you choose. Being psychic means connecting with truth, all, one. Using psychic ability combined with intuition creates an opening within that allows you to experience love or, if you already have, to feel it more deeply than you've ever felt it before.

I want to clarify the difference between a psychic and an intuition coach. A psychic is someone who has the ability to see, hear, feel, and know the past, present, and probable future (no future is set in stone). Some psychics are more gifted in their ability to see spirit. This is called clairvoyance. Other psychics are good at pinpointing information from the past, however they have no ability to see the future. A psychic reads energy. A psychic medium can communicate with spirit guides and loved ones who have passed over. There are far fewer mediums than psychics.

Usually people who go to psychics want to be told what is going to happen in their lives. A good psychic will present the information to you and give you suggested next steps. The problem comes when you are receiving a reading from someone who doesn't have an understanding or access to knowledge that will create solutions for you.

I decided to provide support as an intuition coach even though I'm a psychic medium because I want to empower you to trust yourself. I want to show you how to trust your intuition. An intuition coach taps into information in other planes of consciousness and gives you specific steps to follow so that you do not procrastinate or get stuck in overwhelm because you don't already have a plan in place. A good intuition coach guides you to find your own answers and develop a deep sense of trust within yourself. Stop handing your power away. You can be your own intuition coach today and tap into the psychic realms, to support yourself in life.

Deep Healing

The purpose of *Unleash the Psychic in You* is inner healing. No woo-woo healing. No quick fix. Healing in the true sense is about creating a strong connection to your soul. When you feel hurt or broken, your energy fragments. It can feel as if pieces of your soul have been lost or are stuck out in the universe beyond reach. The reason a piece broke off is predominantly that you did not value that part of your soul or your ego exiled it because someone else rejected it. You can retrieve those parts of self. All the parts of you that were fragmented by broken hearts, financial losses, betrayals, or wasted time can be retrieved and reintegrated. It's not too late for you to experience wholeness.

Once you achieve wholeness, the challenge is maintaining it. With mindfulness and diligent practice you can live a life of joy, happiness and aliveness.

I recommend you read this book with an open mind and heart. Notice when judgment or resistance kicks in. Observe your emotions. Your unconscious blocks could trigger anger, fear, and sadness. If your skepticism is aroused you may decide that since I am an imperfect human being I am not a valid teacher. The reason someone would want a psychic like me to be perfect is that they're scared to take responsibility for the answers they receive. They don't know what to do next. You have an opportunity to overcome your unconscious fears as you are learning to use your own intuitive gifts. Then you can verify or disprove everything I say for yourself and keep only that which works for you.

I suggest you absorb this information instead of trying to understand it. To gain clarity in your own life, you need to move beyond your consciousness and be aware that your ego will continually lead you away from truth. Allow your intuition to unfold. This is not a race to be psychic or to be more psychic than someone else. What's most important is what you do with the guidance you receive from your intuition. Certain principles will strike more of a chord with you than others. This is your intuition guiding you to channel energy into learning more deeply about how you can apply the life lesson, skill, or technique to your own life.

The more you practice using your intuition, the more inner guidance you shall receive. Happy intuition development!

Chapter 1

The F**ked up Psychic
(How I Lost Everything)

"I feel there are two people inside me—me and my intuition. If I go against her, she'll screw me every time, and if I follow her, we get along quite nicely." —Kim Basinger

As a successful psychic for years I was terrified that someone would find out about the skeletons in my closet. What would people think if they knew I had stayed in a disastrous relationship for six years and lost everything I owned?

Do you remember how Dorothy, Toto, and their friends went on a challenging journey down the Yellow Brick Road to find the Wizard and when they got there, it turned out the Wizard was a little old man hiding behind a curtain? Let's pretend the Wizard is a psychic. Yes, that's me. Let's take a look backstage, behind my curtain.

For three years I asked myself the following question almost every day and sometimes several times a day: "If I'm such a wonderful psychic, why is my life a bloody mess?" It pained me that I could see so clearly for others, and when it came to my own life I had made a series of awful decisions that resulted in me losing everything. I lost my home, car, and all my money (I had a lot). I fell into $100,000 of debt. I had gone from being a strong, independent woman who wouldn't settle for a guy unless he had all the qualities I wanted, to being a severely

1

insecure codependent who bought love with loans and gifts to her boyfriend because I feared no better man would love me if he knew who I really was. I stayed in an unhealthy relationship way past it's expiration date.

What happens when you eat something that's expired? It tastes disgusting and can make you ill. My body gave me repeated warning signs that I needed to leave my relationship pronto. One of these was that I put on a lot of weight. I had always easily fit into size 6 clothing. Then one day my mom took me shopping. I remember we went from boutique to boutique because my butt wouldn't fit into anything I tried on. We ended up in a department store where we finally found some pants and shorts that would fit me. They were a size 10. I was an inch away from being a size 12.

"You never used to be like this. What's happened to you?" Mom asked.

"Nothing, I'm fine. I guess they're making the clothes smaller," I said. Now that's denial with a capital "D." I couldn't see my decline. How had I become so blind?

The Other Side

A few weeks before, I was doing a Reiki healing session with a client of mine who was in a hospital. A tumor had just been removed from her brain. When the nurse came in the room to check on her, I kept hearing a Scottish voice clear as a bell. It said, "Oh Maggie, Maggie, Maggie." I ignored the voice, however an intense feeling, like my heart was going to burst if I didn't speak, swept over me as the nurse went to leave the room. I blurted out, "Do you know someone called Maggie?"

The nurse stopped in her tracks and looked at me suspiciously. "Why do you ask?"

"You'll think it's silly if I tell you," I said. I felt like a total idiot.

"Go on," she said.

I took a deep breath and spoke with my heart down in my stomach. "I sense a woman around you. She cared for you very much and she keeps saying 'Oh, Maggie.' Does this make any sense to you?"

The nurse didn't respond. I was ridiculously embarrassed. Finally she said, "I'm Maggie."

"You are?" I said.

"Only my mother called me Maggie. Everyone else calls me Margaret." Chills shot through me, as tears came to her eyes. I'd gone to the hospital to see my client and here I was acting as a psychic medium for her nurse. This was one of many early medium experiences I had before I was comfortable with my gift. I struggled for a long time to understand the rules of the spirit world. I didn't know what I was meant to do with this ability.

My boyfriend at the time used me as a psychic like someone drinks water. He became more and more reliant on my guidance. He was almost ten years my senior and yet wouldn't decide what to have for breakfast without asking me to check in with his spirit guides first. I let him offload all responsibility for his actions onto me. At first it felt good to be consulted. I felt special, loved, and important. But I was on a slippery slope. Yes, my ego f***ked me up. When things went great for him,

I'd feel wonderful. When they went poorly, my relationship would turn ugly.

People have free will. This means a psychic can only predict a probable future. Things can change. My boyfriend was a control freak and to alleviate his consciousness of causing an undesired outcome, he'd blame me. Here's a typical response from my boyfriend. "You didn't say this would happen. It's your fault that I listened to you."

"Then don't ask," I said.

"You're the psychic," he would reply, almost spitting venom. Ten minutes later he'd ask me to get guidance for him again.

It got to the point where if anything didn't work out in his life he'd dump on me. In his eyes, it was my fault. It took me years to see this was a subtle form of abuse. Sometimes I wish he had hit me because then I would have had bruises as concrete evidence of his abuse and I'd have had a stronger motivation to leave him.

I felt like a golden goose that couldn't lay gold eggs. I allowed my intuition to be abused. Every time I tried to see my next best step, the guidance was distorted because I'd unknowingly shut off my connection to spirit. I thought it would be easier to have no communication with my spirit guides because then my boyfriend would stop asking me what to do every five minutes. But he kept harassing me. In the end I'd say anything to get him off my back. I ate to shut off the pain. My intuitive reservoir was dry. If a drop of water was to be found, my boyfriend drank it.

That's when I began getting severe nosebleeds on a consistent basis. They were another warning sign. I saw a correlation between him asking for guidance, me getting upset, and then five minutes later my nose bleeding like crazy. I was terrified. Yet I still couldn't prove that he was making them happen. It took me two more years to realize that I was the one making these nosebleeds happen, by staying with this self-centered man.

Rock Bottom

My turning point happened on a cold January day back in 2004. I remember it so clearly. Mom and I were sitting in her silver Mercedes C230 Kompressor in front of Harrods department store in London. It's a very famous store that sells the most luxurious brands in the world. In contrast, here I was sitting in Mom's car, financially, mentally, emotionally, and spiritually broke. I'd hit bottom. I felt so ashamed as Mom looked at me that I could barely bring my gaze to meet hers. I felt like a wounded animal trapped in a cage for I sensed what she was about to ask. The interrogation was about to begin.

Only when I later gained clarity did I understand that my mother was devastated by who I had become. She had done her best to give me everything a girl could possibly wish for. She always stocked the fridge full of delicious food, bought me beautiful clothes, and acted as a confidante when I was going through boy trouble. And she was most forgiving of my errors. I had thrown all those gifts away. I'd destroyed and dismissed everything she'd previously given me.

"How are you surviving?" Mom said.

I looked down at my hands and noticed the five-dollar engagement ring I'd bought for myself because my boyfriend, who'd become fiancé, didn't have any money.

"I'm surviving," I said.

"That's never what I wanted your life to be. Where did I go wrong? I gave you everything I could," Mom said.

My heart felt crushed. The deepest sense of remorse I'd ever experienced washed over me and stuck like molasses. "I'm surviving and my fiancé loves me," I said defensively.

"Joanna, you have bills to pay. How are you managing that? How much money do you have?" Mom asked.

I could barely muster enough voice and when I did, it didn't even sound like me. "Thirty pence," I said. (In dollars, that's sixty cents).

Mom scoffed. I could see she was trying to grasp how I'd gone from a hip London party girl who owned her own home (today worth over a million dollars), and had held excellent jobs in entertainment PR and corporate finance.

"How are you going to eat?" Mom said.

"I don't know," I said.

"Joanna, you're over thirty years old. You're approaching middle age."

I sat in silence. I dreaded facing anyone. The thought of my friends seeing me like this made me feel so ashamed.

"I can't help you. You got yourself in this mess. Get yourself out of it. I'm going to Australia for three weeks. If you're still living with this loser when I get back, I don't want anything to do with you — and I know Daddy feels the same way. There's nothing more we can do to help you," Mom said.

Mom opened her Louis Vuitton handbag and took out her purse. She handed me five pounds.

"Thank you," I said sheepishly.

This was money to pay for the subway back to the oppressively small, starkly decorated basement apartment of my fiancé's mom. It had no heating or hot water because the thermostat had broken. The woman was away in India and was letting me stay there because she felt awful that her son owed me $400,000.

I wrestled with the lock to the apartment door for ten minutes before getting in from the cold. I made myself a cup of tea and ate a piece of toast with strawberry jam before sitting down to call the temping agencies for secretarial work. In the past I'd been Executive Assistant to the Managing Director of Saatchi & Saatchi and to the Senior Vice President of Goldman Sachs. One agency out of seven now replied to my résumé. Two days later I was scheduled for only one interview in the West End in central London, except I didn't have enough money for the train or the bus to get there. My only option was to walk to my 10:30 A.M. appointment. I MapQuested the address and saw I'd be walking five miles. I put on sneakers and placed my smarter shoes in a plastic bag. I did my best to remain optimistic as I climbed the three flights of stairs to the temp agency's office. Quickly I changed my shoes and put on my brightest, most confident smile.

A young woman in her twenties dressed in a conservative suit and heels led me into a small room with a computer for my typing test. I scored 100 percent on my spelling test and had a typing speed of seventy words per minute. I was pleased to see I hadn't lost my skills. I went through the motions of explaining why I'd be a good candidate and gave my credentials to the interviewer. "We'll be in touch," she said.

As I changed back into my sneakers on the street around the corner from the agency, I prayed, "Please God, let me get a job." Ten pounds an hour would feel like winning the lottery. Then it began to rain and rain hard. A voice inside my head said "Don't give up, it's never too late." I felt I had nothing more to lose. What harm would it be to take a detour to Regent's College on the grounds of The Regent's Park?

I had a healing client in Cheltenham, Jules Williams, a fantastic celebrity TV psychic who is now my dear friend. His challenge at the time was to break through his block of canceling a workshop when only three people had registered. He always cancelled it before anyone else could sign up because his limiting belief was, "No one is really interested in my knowledge." Jules didn't know at the time that I had my own crap to deal with or how messed up and insecure I was, because I acted bright and confident.

A few days earlier we'd sat in a little coffee shop together and I'd said, "Jules let's host a workshop together and break this pattern." Now here I was down at Regent's College checking out the venue for this potential live event. I told myself all the reasons not to do the workshop. "If the room's awful, we'll cancel the event." Except the room was wonderful with a view of majestic trees. The space felt peaceful and serene. I phoned

8

Jules. "We've got to do this psychic development workshop. The venue is amazing."

As I walked through The Regent's Park, I felt hopeful for the first time in ages, even though fear lurked beneath. I ignored it and did my best to control my small black umbrella, as it flapped in the driving rain. A glimmer of intuition got my attention for the first time in ages. "Go back to school," my intuition said. I took that literally. My old school, Francis Holland, was just beyond the grounds of The Regent's Park.

I turned up without an appointment. My timing was perfect. The teachers were about to take a coffee break. The school secretary led me up to the staff room and my former Italian teacher, Mr. Cicora, handed me a cup of coffee with a cookie. I was surrounded by several of my teachers. They bombarded me with questions. "What have you achieved since you left school? Are you married?"

I explained I was engaged. "Let's see the ring," someone chimed.

I tried to deflect the request, because the ring was unimpressive, and racked my brain for an achievement. "I produced a movie that got a nationwide release."

I wanted to get the focus off of me because I felt like a fraud.

"Well you'd be perfect to judge the school drama competition in three weeks. Tom Stoppard did it last year; his daughter goes to the school. But he's not available this year. Would you be willing to step in?" the school vice president said.

Tom Stoppard, the playwright? Are you kidding me? Surely, I would make a complete fool of myself. "Yes, of course, I'd love to," I said.

Lights, Camera, Action

It was now February and the day of the drama competition had arrived. Mrs. Low, the headmistress of the school, invited me into her office to give me a run-through of events. When I entered the assembly, the entire school was present as I was introduced as the special guest judge in front of 300 people, including all my old teachers. I hid my fear well. I took notes as I watched the plays performed by each class, and all the while Mrs. Low by my side. As the afternoon progressed, I discovered that I was the only judge. There was no panel. What if I made the wrong choices?

The school was delighted with my selection of winners. I was invited up on stage and presented with a beautiful bouquet of flowers and a book certificate. Everyone stood up and applauded me. I was surprised. I'd been beaten down for so long that this felt foreign to me, but it also felt good. It didn't matter that I hadn't heard from the temp agency at that moment. I heard a voice say very gently but firmly in my head, "All is well, you will see." The voice was so reassuring. It stopped me falling any deeper into self-pity when I didn't hear from the employment agency.

The following weekend, Jules and I hosted our psychic development workshop at Regent's College for fourteen people. It was a success and the attendees went on to sign up for our next event. Even more importantly, taking this small step to commit to the workshop led to me producing and hosting on TV.

Before the workshop I remember thinking, "What the hell. I'm just going to call people and let them know about the workshop and they can say no if they want to. But they may say yes." I called a young woman named Eddy for whom I'd given a psychic reading a year before in a pub in West London. She said, "That's so weird you should call because I was about to call you. I'm working for a production company and they want to make a psychic TV show." She continued, "We've been interviewing all these psychics and they're awful. I think you could be perfect for this."

When you're attuned to your life purpose everything flows. It's not weird. It's what author James Redfield calls synchronicity in *The Celestine Prophecy*.

A couple of days later, I walked down Great Portland Street with greasy hair because I couldn't face putting my head under a freezing cold shower. I was headed to the TV studio. Once there, the receptionist didn't direct me to a boardroom. Instead, she sent me to a pub across the street. The person that hired me didn't even test my psychic skills. He looked at me and said, "You'll do." The following week I was given the task of hosting a show and creating ten hours of live psychic television programming a week. It became an international success and went on to make its producers millions of dollars.

In March 2004, my engagement abruptly ended. My ex-fiancé turned up at my friend's apartment where I was staying unannounced. "Mom's away and I've only got nineteen and a half pence, could you lend me thirty pounds to get the train back to Cheltenham?" he asked. I felt numb. I took forty pounds out of my purse that I'd just earned from doing my TV show and handed it to him. He spent the night. We took the subway to Oxford Circus together the following morning. I was headed to the TV studio. He was on his way to approach some commercial agencies for directing jobs. This time, we didn't kiss each other goodbye.

Destructive Expectations

Before my turning point, I had lost everything I owned because I didn't value myself. I justified giving away my time and skills for very little money or for free. That's not so unusual. I see many people doing this to themselves, not only psychics. But many people in my life thought that because being psychic is a gift it should be given away for free, and I went along with them. For many years I did psychic readings for free and got burned out in the process. My soul didn't feel nourished. Would a doctor, actor or singer be expected to work for no pay? So why should psychic readings be done at no charge?

I have heard so much uproar about what psychics charge, probably because there is such a serious exploitation of the sixth sense. Psychic phone lines offering you instant solutions can easily swallow all your money. If you're tempted to dial in, be aware that the psychics that get hired for these phone companies are like battery hens churning out egg after egg, so their advice is far from golden. This way of using the sixth sense is not the answer. Do you know what the turnover of psychics is at a psychic phone line? Approximately every two weeks, they need to replace each person. Go look online. They often use fake IDs. Are you sure the voice on the other end of the phone is the person you saw in the photo online?

As for the rest of us, usually the complaint is that we charge too much. But rates vary. An individual psychic's fees have got nothing to do with being psychic. What you charge is all about how you value your time. There are only so many hours in the day and if someone wants to consult with you and they value your time and your worth, you have the right to charge whatever you want. Psychics are not priests. We're are not seers or prophets sitting around on mountaintops anymore. We live in the twenty-first century.

People are funny about psychics. I've worked with clients who expected me to be dressed head to toe in white and virginal. I've met witches who got into a rivalry with me: "I'm more psychic than you. I can intimidate you with my psychic powers and turn you into a frog." Oh please! Everyone has psychic ability. Psychic is a label that's old. One of the reasons I got into trouble in my life was that I was always worried about what people thought of me. I allowed their beliefs about who I should be and how I should use my gift run my life. Obviously that didn't work.

The main reason I lost everything I owned was because I took on the following belief from my ex-fiancé, "You can't have money and be spiritual." I became ashamed of all my beautiful possessions. Of course my fiancé didn't object to me buying him clothes at Giorgio Armani, a new laptop computer, or flying him first class to a luxury five-star resort. I was buying love and slowly but surely my guilt about it began to consume me.

When I first started dating my ex-fiancé, my Dad invited us for a luxury vacation at a spa in Evian (yes, where the water comes from). It is one of the most divine places I've stayed in my life. The entire time my boyfriend kept dropping the comment "You're such a daddy's girl." "No I'm not," I replied sheepishly, as another level of shame kicked in. I wanted to be perceived as a strong, independent woman who didn't need anything from anyone. I wanted to have all the answers for all the wrong reasons.

At dinner one evening, boyfriend called my dad, "A redneck fascist." It was awful. I lost a part of my soul that night because I was ashamed of the strong bond I had with Dad. I disconnected from my father and to bury the pain, I kept loaning more and more money to boyfriend. "I'll pay you back soon," he said. This became his mantra. All the while, I kept loaning. I loaned and spent on boyfriend until I had no more. And in the process I became disconnected from myself. I numbed my heart because I couldn't bear to face the path I was heading down. I knew I was going further and further off track.

At night I'd go to bed and pray, "God, help me please?" As the months went by, I became angrier and angrier with God because I thought, "God is doing this to me and I should be saved." This is where people typically go wrong. And this is how I fell apart. I had no sense of responsibility, no awareness, no boundaries, and no self-love.

Ignoring my gut instinct was the worst thing I could do to myself. That expression, "Ignorance is bliss," is nonsense. Some people wonder why they have mediocre lives. They think they are at the mercy of others and they love being the martyr. Yes, I was a big, cuddly martyr. Being a martyr doesn't serve anyone. It is the nemesis of gut instinct. When I put my gut instinct on the shelf, my boundaries went out the window. I attracted the wrong types of friendships. I missed great job opportunities. I gave away too many good ideas. I didn't get paid my worth. Can you relate?

Have you experienced overwhelm, a dead-end relationship that isn't nurturing your soul, a boring job, or a one-sided friendship? The good news is you can stop that now. You can change your choices. It's never too late. My darkest hour led me to increased clarity. The pain I put myself through helped me truly understand what respect is and how to give that to all human beings, including myself. I learned that being a doormat and a people-pleaser made me ineffective and useless.

Today, I have more clarity about who I am. Everyone has an opinion. It doesn't have to become my belief. Some people want to project their beliefs onto others because it makes them feel part of the herd. Marriage, for instance, gives a false sense of security, and that's why many marriages don't last. They are built on making another person happy. In recent years I've learned to love and be giving, all the while maintaining my own truth. Just because someone says something, "Is," doesn't mean it is, "So."

By the way, that includes what I share here. Check everything I say. I only wish that you apply and meditate upon what feels good to you. If something I share triggers you. I suggest you look at it more deeply. Whenever I feel reactive, it's an indicator to me that I'm tapping into a past boundary violation that is being reactivated. This may be an old wound or a warning that I'm about to go swim with sharks. Now I get out of the water every time without question. That's what happens when you trust your intuition.

Bright Shiny Psychic Syndrome

Since I was six years old I can remember being psychic. I only started to pursue studying my intuition when I turned twenty-one. Actually my spirit guides were trying to navigate me in the right direction and I repeatedly ignored their wisdom, so it's more like I dragged myself into studying it. I thought being psychic was something that just happened. I assumed that because I could see an aura or energy that my life would run smoothly and I wouldn't have to do anything else because I was connected to God. Seeing spirit, hearing dead people, and feeling people's energy doesn't mean you make the best choices. Being psychic only means you have an active sixth sense.

The sixth sense, which is another name for intuitive sensing, which takes place beyond the five physical senses, gives you a heightened perception of reality. Intuition is what you need to use to know what steps to take in reality. Reality is your life. Having the ability of clairvoyance, meaning "to see clearly," simply confirms you can perceive other dimensions, like an X-ray. It's what the doctor does with the X-ray that is important. When I became actively clairvoyant, I'd spend hours watching energy. A friend would sit with me in my home and I'd say, "I can see you whole energy body and you have a guide next to you."

"What is the guide doing?" my friend would ask.

"It's standing to your left," I said.

"Does it want to tell me something?"

"I don't know," I said.

I was lazy and I was missing the point. I was so caught up in the sensationalism of seeing what other people couldn't easily see that I failed to recognize my gift's healing potential. It was bright, shiny object syndrome that was dazzling me.

When I was casting the psychic TV show in London, I interviewed many other psychics. I'd psychically read them while they gave me a psychic reading. Pretty exhausting! One psychic, who was considered one of the best in the world, was a fabulous example of psychic sensationalism. Here's a sneak peek of the reading:

"I see a red sports car. Do you know someone with a red sports car?" the psychic asked.

"No," I said.

"Do you know someone with a sports car?" the psychic asked.

"Yes," I said.

"A boyfriend?" the psychic asked.

"No," I said.

"Who?" the psychic asked.

"My Dad," I said.

"Okay, he has a message for you and you're going to meet someone with a red sports car," the psychic said.

Spirit will often give images clairvoyantly as a code to gain deeper insight. The psychic took this image literally. I want to share some more of this experience with you.

"You wear big hats," the psychic said.

"No," I said.

"You're getting married," the psychic said.

"No, I just split up with someone," I said.

"I see you going to Tunisia," the psychic said.

"You do?" I asked.

"Yes, you'll be going to a wedding in Tunisia this summer and I see you wearing a big hat," the psychic said.

I'm not kidding! See what I mean about exploitation of the sixth sense? Just because a psychic says you'll do something doesn't necessarily make it true. You have free will. A psychic can see your probable future. That future definitely wasn't mine.

There's more.

"Do you know someone whose name begins with the letter "D?" the psychic asked.

"Dad?"

"Yes, go call him afterwards. There's something he needs to tell you," the psychic said.

And finally the piece de resistance, "My guides are telling me to tell you it's time to go to the dentist," the psychic said.

There is a vast amount of symbolism in clairvoyance. It takes time to build your own psychic dictionary. You will definitely face a period of trial and error as you move through your psychic development. Some psychics don't want to take the time to learn the communication skills of how to work with spirit guides and translate the meaning of energy into everyday life. Many psychics are not held accountable because some people put psychics on a pedestal. They think, "I can ignore the elephant in the room because a psychic is here." Then denial rains on everyone.

I didn't realize the importance of intuition. It took me a long time to see that intuitive development is the necessary foundation for the successful application of the psychic impressions you receive to improve your life. Most successful entrepreneurs I've interviewed don't think they are psychic, however they swear by their gut instinct. That's intuition. Follow your intuition and it will lead you to success.

A Different Paradigm

It took me years to understand that not everyone saw or felt what I was experiencing. I assumed that everyone had abilities like mine. I thought it was normal. When I was six and on vacation in Miami with my family I got myself into a lot of trouble by speaking the truth of what I saw. An eleven-year-old boy said something to a girl that I knew was a lie. I could see his true intentions in the form of energy. I interjected and said what I knew. The boy pushed me down the stairs.

It took me a while to learn that speaking the truth could get me hurt. And not just by being physically assaulted by little boys. I ended up internalizing the energy of all the lies I was exposed to. I'd hear them spoken, feel the pain of the distorted energy, and then absorb that pain into my body. Eating helped alleviate this pain. When I was younger I think my parents thought I was eccentric and sensitive.

When I started delve deeper into my intuition and participating in the world of professional psychics, my mother thought I was going nuts and my dad found it amusing. Both my parents are grounded, smart, and practical. My mom finds it hard to relate to what I do, but she accepts it. She has very strong intuition herself, but she thinks that's normal. She keeps me from getting caught up in sensationalism. Dad and I are energetically connected. We often call or text-message each other at the same time. We have a lot of synchronicity occur, as we are in tune with each other. I think Dad is highly clairsentient, meaning he is sensitive to energy and feeling people's feelings. Now that I'm out the other side of my craziness, I have an excellent relationship with my parents. They are supportive and encouraging of my work.

For years after breaking up I continued to beat myself up emotionally for staying in a destructive relationship. I was brilliant at guiding other people in relationships and when it came to myself I drew a total blank. I stayed in that relationship because I'm an idealist. I always want to focus on the best in everyone. That led me to denial. But it wasn't only in this one relationship that I had trouble. For a period of several years, the more my psychic abilities increased, the more blind I became.

When you open to your intuitive side, energy, thoughts, and patterns that have run like clockwork and taken you through life on autopilot begin to rise to the surface of your consciousness. It can be very distressing to see them. It's human nature to want to keep things as they are. We don't like change and so our impulse is to get rid of pain with a quick fix. As you experience more light and clarity in your life when you are entering into an accelerated spiritual growth cycle, the opposite polarity of darkness and confusion will happen simultaneously. This is an excellent indicator that a negative cycle of patterns is about to be broken. The biggest mistake people make when this happens is to go backwards. This is very common, but if people recognize it they can bolster their resolve and keep going forwards. Sometimes when I am about to release an old wound from inside of me, I'll get scared and slip back into my comfort zone, which actually is uncomfortable. I only have the courage to change my behavior when the pain inside me becomes excruciating. This happens less and less now that I'm aware of this pattern.

I often get asked how I became a professional intuition coach. I'd have to say I was always psychic. But there were also elements in my background that opened me up to these gifts, which I believe you also possess. For instance, I was always asking questions about the meaning of existence. Why I am here? Where do we come from? I also was surrounded by diversity and was fortunate to be brought up in an open environment. I never took anything on face value. I always sought my own guidance.

When I was six, I used to kneel down by the side of my bed with my hands clasped in front of me and my eyes closed, and I would pray. I did this every night and as a result I had powerful dreams. I remember some of those dreams like I dreamed them yesterday. I was fascinated by the parables in the Old Testament and the New Testament. I read them often. I'm Jewish, but I attended a Christian school growing up. I couldn't understand why other kids didn't have dreams like me. At times I found it hard to relate to them. I felt shut out and alone. But I also felt fortunate to grow up in a liberal environment. I gained insight about many religions in my home, in school, and from the people in my neighborhood.

I grew up in a beautiful five-bedroom house in a cul-de-sac in Hampstead, which is in the northwest of London. Our house was surrounded by several homes whose inhabitants were ambassadors from Trinidad, Tobago, Iran, Holland, Papua New Guinea, China, Sri Lanka, and the United States. It was great because there were kids growing up in each of these homes so I was immersed in a palette of different religions. I believe God is like a different language for each religion. God presents the same messages, however each person, culture, country has its own unique slant on these. God is the one energy that we all have as a common thread.

I used to think God was a man about seventy years old who had long white hair and a beard, and dressed in simple iridescent white robes. Today I experience God as an all-pervading energy. When I'm in a state of heightened attunement, God just is. God is a collective consciousness. Everyone is God. I believe God created us all equal. I didn't always experience God this way, or feel clarity and love to the degree that I now do. There were many times in my life when I felt disconnected from God's love.

When I was going through my struggles my prayers were needy and desperate. I'd pray, "Why don't you rescue me?" Although I prayed to God, it was not in gratitude. I prayed when I thought I needed something and I stopped praying when things went well. Even though I felt abandoned, I was the one abandoning myself. I cut my connection to consciously experiencing God. I have studied for many years the cause and effect relationship of our thoughts. There is a direct correlation between our thoughts and the things that are happening in our lives. Our lack of awareness about this correlation distorts our perception of reality, makes us feel like victims, and prevents us from being able to experience truth and clarity.

You'll only get as much out of developing your intuition as you put in. If you only dip your toe in your pool of consciousness, you're not going to get wet. Dive in or shut up. All the times I prayed for the right relationship, success, and true happiness, I didn't get what I'd wanted because I was allowing myself to be unconscious and irresponsible.

It's important that you take responsibility for your own spiritual development. Angels and spirit guides can be pretty tough when giving spiritual guidance. They don't tell you what you want to hear. They tell you what you need to know. People who ask for guidance often don't get this, and then they wonder why they're stuck.

If you pray to God or go to church every Sunday and you are still dissatisfied with your lot in life, it's evident to me that your prayers do not come from a loving intention. When you pray from a place of acceptance and gratitude, even if you feel things are going poorly in your life you will feel a sense of peace along with the pain. That's how you know you are in alignment with God's will and that you are living your life purpose.

I have come to accept that my life purpose is to help people open up to their own intuition. When I began my journey along the psychic pathway, I was so caught up in the bells and whistles of the psychic world that I lost sight of what I was supposed to be doing with my ability. When I began my psychic development training, I was doing it for superficial reasons. I wanted to be loved. I wanted people to say, "Wow, she's special." I was competitive. I was a great student and the teacher's pet. But I totally missed the point of why my soul was guiding me along this Yellow Brick Road. Thus I was blind when I read for myself. I got caught up in the Great Mystery without experiencing any greatness because I was only a talented novice who needed to get her skill and purpose in check, and learn to be more consistent in connecting daily with God.

When I learned the difference between humility and low self-esteem, I gained clarity and became who I am now. I let myself off the hook. I stopped being the martyr. I didn't take on other people's pain anymore. As the weight of the pain lifted from me, an abundance of knowledge and understanding became available to me. I'm proud of the work I do. I'm grateful that I have the opportunity to witness people's godliness blossom. When clients phone me or email me with news that they've met "The One," got their dream role in a movie, or they repaired a relationship with an estranged parent, my heart leaps in joy. This is what keeps me going, and this is what I want to share with you.

A distinction in my professional career as an intuition coach is that I help show my clients how to gain their own clarity. I've learned that it is more powerful to guide people to find their own answers than to ask me to provide them with information, because this leads to long-lasting positive change. Most psychics tell people what their problems are and give suggestions for improvements, however their clients don't have the tools to confirm the guidance or to make the change. The risk is that clients may not understand and therefore will stay stuck after the feeling of relief from the psychic reading has subsided.

People often think of the sixth sense as an ability that you are or aren't born with. Your sixth sense is a combination of six heightened skills: sight (clairvoyance), sound (clairaudience), touch (clairsentience), knowing (claircognizance), smell (clairolfactory), and taste (clairgustation). Each one of these skills has a varying perspective to give you regarding any situation in your life about which you need guidance.

When I'm giving a response to a client's question in a reading, I'll often hear the answer first, however I won't speak the guidance until I've checked in with what I'm feeling through my clairsentience and also received visual concepts or pictures in my mind's eye. Having three sources of confirmation leads me to the feeling of knowing, after which I will share the information I have received. This all happens very quickly. I can simultaneously separate out and distinguish the message from each intuitive sense. This ability didn't happen overnight for me.

The key was to practice each one of these skills separately and then put them all together. That helped me develop confidence.

We all have the ability to access psychic guidance. You just have to believe.

Chapter 2

MEET MY BEST FRIEND, SHE'S CALLED "INTUITION"

"The only real valuable thing is intuition." —*Albert Einstein*

In·tu·i·tion *(in-too-ish-on) n. 1. quick and ready insight 2. the power or faculty of attaining to direct knowledge or cognition without evident rational thought and inference.* —*Dictionary.com*

Intuition is inner guidance. Intuition is your internal teacher. Intuition is your treasure map to all the gold your heart desires. So why is it so hard to tap into intuition? The only person who makes it challenging is you. Intuition is not hidden. If you're having trouble being intuitive, it is likely that you have unknowingly buried it. Intuition can be veiled by spirit for your protection. Perhaps you need more time to see the truth of your situation. God's path is gentle. It is only ever the ego that intensifies pain and depression.

When you develop your intuition, you begin to perceive thoughts and energy beyond your conscious awareness. Suddenly you have access to another dimension of knowledge and heightened awareness. Imagine you were planning a skiing vacation a year ahead of time and you had the ability to see that there would be no snow for the duration of your stay. Wouldn't you change your plans if your specific intention were

27

to ski? You can apply this kind of foresight to any area of your life now.

Intuition gives you access to the big picture. Using your intuition will help you to see beyond your limiting beliefs, such as "I'll never succeed," "I'm unlovable," "I'm too fat," "I'll be rejected," and "I'm a failure." Having strong intuition makes you self-reliant and more confident. It helps you set healthy boundaries when you don't feel you need to get answers outside of you. It also saves you a lot of time, for instance, because you won't need to phone five different people for their opinion on your situation. It is important to acknowledge the difference between needing to do research to complete a project and calling every single one of your friends to ask them whether or not you should go out on a second date with a guy. Such distractions are a waste of productive time.

When I see people focused on what's wrong with a friend or a family member instead of taking care of their own problems, I know they are in denial. They are stuck and scared. This does not mean to stop being concerned for the people you care about. Just check if these people really sought your advice. Putting your focus on other's lives, problems, and successes takes you right out of your inner awareness. This is the fastest way to disconnect from your intuition. It could make you feel numb and empty.

Intuition gives you laser point focus and clarity. It guides you to take steps that your ego may dislike. Your ego will put up a damn good fight when you begin listening to and acting upon your intuition. It will tell you all the reasons that the guidance of your intuition is bad for you. So don't be surprised if you suddenly feel like you are taking the wrong steps or slipping backwards in your life. Intuition unearths all your poor decisions that have led to painful results. Things can get worse before they get better. The good news is once you place the past in the trash, you can now see all the gems of wise guidance.

When you're intuitive, you exude calm, peace, knowing, and confidence. This causes people to want to be around you more. They sense your energy is magnetic and yet they can't quite put their finger on why. Be aware of the fear that may arise as you feel people being attracted to your newfound strength and clarity. Keep focused on your own guidance and do not be swayed by outside opinions.

Don't go around bragging about how intuitive you are because you're excited by the new results you are getting in your life. You could unknowingly kick intuition out the door. Being externally focused pulls the plug on the inner connection that is like the electric socket providing the energy of intuitive guidance. Pride will kill your intuition.

Intuition development is a dance. It takes time to learn the moves. You're going to tread on intuition's toes, feel embarrassed, and retreat. Go slow. Watch the moves that intuition makes. Stick close. Follow her steps. Relax into her. Let her guide you. Feel the music of intuition. Breathe her in. Allow her to inspire you so that you can stop worrying about doing things right and instead dance your life in a way that can only be described as exhilarating.

Your Intuition Is Never Wrong

The most common question I hear from my students is: "What if my intuition is wrong?" Your intuition is never wrong. It's your ego that misguides you. It takes time to know the voice of your intuition and to be able easily to recognize the tone of your ego.

When you take a step based upon what you believe to be your intuition and things don't work out the way you want, don't beat yourself up. Learn from your mistake. Reflect on why you thought you were being guided by your intuition. Peel back the layers of your true motivation and you'll begin to see what intuition is and what it is not.

If your unconscious mind is running the show and it's out of alignment with your heart's desire, you've got an enemy in your camp. But outing it and punishing it is only going to create chaos. Instead ask this enemy for a private chat. Make it feel special. Treat it like a dear friend. Let your ego open up to you. Your ego wants to be heard. Just because you listen to it doesn't mean you have to do what it says. You're not being deceptive by communicating with your ego and you're not being disloyal to your intuition. You are calming and nurturing the ego. You are healing the pain your ego is experiencing. It's been trying to speak with you for a long time. If you were trying to get someone's attention because there is something you need to share, you'd raise your voice and eventually get frustrated if you were being ignored. The ego is simply pain that has been ignored. It is the hurt and sometimes trauma that is stored in your mind as thoughts, your body as disease, and your spirit as a perceived distortion of life. If you've sidelined your pain for a long time, your ego is going to play havoc with you until it is heard.

How can you recognize the difference between the voice of the ego and the voice of intuition? Your intuition is always giving you higher guidance. If I follow an action and it works well for me, then I know it was my intuition. Whereas if I take an action that I think is based on intuition and it gives me pain, then I know the voice was my ego. If you follow the ego by accident, don't beat yourself up. Learn quickly from a mistake. The more you practice, the easier it will be to see the subtle differences between the guidance of ego versus the guidance of intuition. It's important to clean up the trauma of the past so that the ego gets out of the way of intuition. You can experience different levels and cycles of transformation simultaneously, which sometimes seem to be one thought and experience, yet there can be multiple beliefs going layers deep in the unconscious that have to be dealt with before the clear voice of your intuition can be heard.

A relationship of trust cannot be built overnight. If you choose to practice diving inwards and letting intuition guide you to the damaged parts of yourself, you will heal. Have you ever met someone to whom you took an instant dislike and as you got to know them, you became good friends? In time you will understand that your ego is intuition in disguise. The message of the ego is, "You're out of alignment, get on track."

Commit to Your Intuition Development

Intuition isn't a dress that you pull out of the closet on special occasions. I want you to use intuition as if it was your favorite pair of walking shoes. Don't worry about intuition being resilient enough to get you to your destination. Just put your shoes on and start walking like Dorothy in *The Wizard of Oz* with her magical red shoes. You know your next best step. It's inside you. Stop thinking about what you need to do next. Open yourself to the flow of your life. Your intuition needs to be exercised.

When you want to get in great physical shape, you don't go to the gym once or twice and then expect to have lost thirty pounds. You have to be consistent. You decide what parts of your body you want to improve and how many days a week you need to work out to get the desired result.

It's exactly the same with your intuition. It can feel like an intense workout when you first practice intuitive development. I remember when I first began weight training; I could barely lift five-pound dumbbells because I had such little upper body strength. Now I can lift twenty-pound weights. My arms would quiver and shake whenever I increased the weight, sometimes I thought I couldn't do it but I did. It's the same for your intuition. At first you are going to be a bit shaky if you haven't used this "muscle" before.

Don't give up because you can't lift the twenty-pound weight yet. Build up to it. Be consistent in your practice. Give yourself breaks. If you keep pushing yourself when you are not ready to go to that next level, you'll give up for good and then you'll only be cheating yourself out of the life you deserve.

I remember going to the gym when I was out of shape and comparing myself to women who were fitness models and had been working out three hours a day for many years. When I did this I felt like shit. My energy would drop and my workout would suffer. The rule in intuition development is to focus on yourself. Feel your own energy and don't tell yourself you're a failure when you can't get the intuitive connection you know you have inside you, right away. It will come. Patience and practice will pay dividends. Commit to a weekly schedule of intuition development and eventually it will become a natural part of your life. You'll find that your intuition can run on autopilot.

Go with Your Intuitive Flow

The key to intuition working successfully in your life is integrating it into everything you do. I use my intuition to turn bad habits into good routines. For instance, whenever I used to feel rejected I'd get on the phone to a friend and complain, whine, or bitch about the situation. Now if I feel an ounce of rejection, I sit with my energy. I ask myself what triggered the reaction (feeling rejected) and I pinpoint what the emotion is and where it is in my body. Then I ask for inner guidance of what I need to do to release the pain. I follow that guidance to the letter. I have transformed numerous bad habits simply by observing myself as I'm going about my day. Intuition gives you an overview of what's really happening. It's like I have a best friend who is watching my back to make sure I don't screw up.

I know I'm applying my intuition when I am calm and centered. When I can understand a person's motivation or a situation from multiple perspectives without judgment, I know I'm in tune. When I act from intuition, I take balanced steps. I know I am taking the right action because I feel connected to my heart. Insecurity and fear recede and knowing is experienced from the deepest part that I am aware of inside of me.

Until you feel this, you won't understand fully, but with inner focus you will receive powerful guidance. How will you know it is correct guidance? It will have a quietly confident resonance to it that is expansive in nature. You are tapping into source energy and the highest aspects of your spirit.

I continually practice listening to my intuition and feeling it in every area of my life, for example while driving in my car, having a conversation, exercising, responding to people's requests, and considering business opportunities. Intuition underscores everything I do.

It wasn't always like that. You will find that you have moments of being totally plugged into your intuition and then suddenly you'll experience a disconnect. This comes from getting caught in fear about making wrong choices or worrying about what others may think or seeking outside approval. Go easy. Apply your intuition to simple, low stakes choices initially. Step outside of your comfort zone gradually. If you try and do too much too quickly, fear will slap you, and then your ego will run the show. Baby steps along the intuitive path will become big strides until eventually you'll be in flow, carried along by the current of invisible energy that is God.

Intuition with Benefits

For some people the thought of using their intuition is daunting. They rationalize away any potential benefits. That rationalization is coming from the ego. In truth, trusting and acting upon intuition has many personal rewards. The foremost reward is that intuition eliminates drama from your life. It gives you awareness to spot a troublemaker from a mile away. Usually troublemakers, drama queens, and energy vampires aren't aware that they are causing chaos, upsetting you, wasting your time, or draining you.

The great thing about strong intuition is you can see the difference between someone who is unconsciously causing craziness in your life and someone who is so insecure that they are consciously trying to hurt you. With someone who is unknowingly hurting you, a compassionate approach is available to you via the application of intuition. A different set of emotional responses comes into play when you realize the person in front of you causing you irritation has a blind spot. Instead of feeling anger towards this person, you find yourself being compassionate. Thus you can maintain the relationship. With a malicious person, your intuition will show you how to shut them down and get away. Your intuition will also show you how to communicate peacefully and plant a seed of healing in a person who is feeling extremely insecure or pained.

This doesn't mean you let the person creating the craziness walk all over you. You now have the opportunity to instead respond with openness, kindness, and clarity because you see their intention. When you respond in this way, you help break the other person's negative pattern because you are not jumping into their cycle of pain. Drama stays on the stage and out of your life if you are not playing the ego game.

When you use your intuition in this way, you may experience incredibly intimate relationships. A marriage that has lost its luster can take on a new depth of love and support. You also can bypass office politics and focus on being creative in your career. Overwhelm and frustration will disappear because you are no longer at the mercy of other people's thought process and actions.

Friends, family, and loved ones will respect you more because you are not allowing yourself to be pulled into their whirlwind of beliefs. When you trust your intuition, you stay centered in the eye of their storms. When people say to you, "He won't listen," "She'll never change," or "You can't get what you want," remember that's their belief and that, yes, it's real for them. Don't react, don't explain, just listen to your intuition.

Let it guide you to a communication that will be a win-win for everyone.

Some people have the win-lose mindset deeply ingrained into their psyches. There is always an alternative if you look at things from a new perspective. Imagine being trapped in a room with no windows or doors. As you look around you, there appears to be no way out. Except when you look up, you notice a faint outline of a rectangle on the ceiling. You push it and a latch releases, and you find a ladder fixed to the panel. All you have to do is climb it and you're free.

Intuition is saying, "Open up. The answers are there. The guidance is available. Look where you haven't looked before. Look inwards."

Your Six Senses

Let's delve a little deeper into the specific qualities of intuition. Because it is not a physical sense, such as taste, smell, touch, sight, and hearing, intuition is often referred to as the "sixth sense." Most people think intuition is gut instinct. Actually there is more to it than that. There are several ways that your intuition could reveal itself, which involve the five senses and an intangible heart knowing.

Anyone who has seen the movie *The Sixth Sense* will remember the line, "I see dead people." There is a big misconception that is "If I can't see dead people, then I'm not psychic." That isn't true. Seeing dead people is one aspect of *clairvoyance*, which is the ability to see beyond what you see with your eyes. Your sixth sense is so much more than that. It is hearing the thoughts of others and the voice of your soul. It is feeling other people's energy inside of you. People who have this aspect of their sixth sense strongly developed are referred to as *sensitives* and *empaths*. It is also knowing the truth before it is so. You know because you know; this intuitive awareness comes from your core.

An acute sense of smell allows you to intuit when there is negative or unresolved energy in your surroundings. A foul smell will act as a warning to be alert. A beautiful scent will often confirm the presence of spirit guides and angels.

Heightened taste is also an intuitive skill. A warning may be given to you through the sudden taste of metal or foulness in your mouth. A sweet taste is confirmation that your spirit guides are trying to convey a message to you.

These are the basic ways that your intuition will speak to you. Your intuition goes layers deep. In fact it is infinite. A good intuitive will never be complacent where they are in their development. However they may rest at a certain level and take reprieve in this place for a while before entering into the next phase of awareness.

People who think they know it all just because they've seen an aura are never going to understand or experience the truth of intuition or its full power. There are psychics out there who have this temperament. Beware of them. Why rely on someone else's poor guidance when you can trust your own heart?

If the concept of intuition development is entirely new to you, it need not overwhelm you. Everyone has to start somewhere. This isn't a race, there's nothing to prove unless your ego is in charge. There's no level you have to get to that confirms you've, "arrived." This is a lifelong experience.

Your first step is accepting that intuition exists. Entertain the possibility that there is energy and intelligence beyond the objects and people we see before our eyes. Don't try and use your intuition, instead observe your surroundings with greater focus. Listen carefully to what people say. This is where you will find intuition. Stop stuffing yourself with food, taking drugs, or dating bad boys or naughty girls when you feel pain arise from within. Don't write off the wisdom of your inner knowing.

Start thinking of yourself as an intuitive being while you live your life. The worst thing you could do is take yourself out of your daily experience. Introspection is good for you, however I've seen some people who became so addicted to meditating that they disconnected from the outside world. They found it hard to be grounded and present in their bodies, and stopped taking responsibility for the practical details of their lives. When this happens, relationships, careers, and finances can fall apart. So be aware that you need to open your intuition gently with the intention of maintaining balance in all aspects of your life, whether these are material or spiritual. With practice, you will develop a heightened sense of awareness.

Intuition Development Meditation Techniques

The simplest and most effective way to awaken your intuition is through silent meditation. There are many types of meditation, including guided meditation and visualization. You will find that some techniques resonate with you more than others. This form of meditation—silent meditation—may be done lying down, seated, or walking.

No matter which way you choose to practice, during silent meditation you do not do activities or tasks where you need to speak with someone. There's no music, no TV, just you. When you quiet the outer voices and external messages on your radio and TV, you give yourself a chance to hear the voice in your head. As you listen, you will begin to notice your thoughts. You may begin to feel uncomfortable because an overwhelming amount of noisy ideas can be running in your mind. This is always happening. We have a lot of information to digest, filter, and discard on a daily basis. Except once you hit the mute button on the external noise now you're aware of it.

Observe how many times you want to go back to listening to the external noise so that you won't have to address what's happening inside of you. Notice if you make excuses about being too busy. But don't let that stop you. We're all too busy and we always will be. You have to create the space for a meditation practice if you're serious about wanting to get results. Also be aware that you will have a very different experience each time you do a silent meditation lying down, sitting, or walking.

Let's look at these three techniques in turn.

Reclining Meditation: An afternoon meditation done lying in the yoga pose called *Shivasana* (aka the corpse position) in Sanskrit will help you to gain access to your higher mind. To do this pose, lie on your back with your feet one- to two-feet apart and extend your arms out to your sides, about a foot away from your hips. If you choose to lie down while you are exhausted, you may fall asleep. However, if you set the intention at the beginning of your session of being in a meditative state, your unconscious mind will begin to clear the internal thoughts while you sleep. You will find you have more energy and clarity when you awaken. Making a conscious choice of how you approach meditation is powerful and deeply healing for your subtle energy fields.

Seated Meditation: You will get your strongest results if you meditate in a seated posture because this posture helps to intensify and expand energy. To do it, sit in a cross-legged position with a straight back, hands facing up or down on the thighs, and eyes closed. The seated pose is most challenging because as the energy intensifies, you may feel uncomfortable in your skin, nauseated, distracted, or fidgety, especially if you have a lot of unprocessed excess energy. Do your best to sit with the energy. Take a few deep breaths in through the nose and out through the mouth to break down the stagnant energy in your body. If the energy feels too intense, move your head a couple of times in a circular motion clockwise, then counter-clockwise. You can also extend your arms out to shoulder height, flex your hands, and then sweep both arms in a circular motion over your head several times before placing your palms facing upwards on your thighs again.

Walking Meditation: Walking meditation is an excellent choice if you're having a tough day or you've been sitting in front of a computer for many hours. The way walking becomes a meditation is to approach it from a state of awareness. This is an opportunity to make your mind alert by noticing how you feel internally during each step you take in any type of environment. As you move into inner awareness, you become more sensitive to everything that surrounds you. Your senses will heighten. You may begin to see things differently. Sounds can take on a new meaning. You will be able to feel what's really happening in your body. If you are depleted, walking meditation will activate a natural healing process. Any time you stop forcing your mind to take action, the body's natural intuition does its job better.

Don't be fooled by the simplicity of these three silent meditation practices. They are extremely powerful when done with mindfulness and intention, and will result in the awakening of your intuition. After years of meditation, I find myself most drawn to these meditations, because as I've become more intuitive I've found more and more gems of wisdom revealed to me through them. Simple techniques are often the most profound.

As you investigate intuition and open to it's potential, you may find that your sixth sense is spontaneously activated. This feels like a deep sense of knowing and understanding, like peace is washing over you. As you become more sensitive to magnetic energy that you were not aware of before, it can feel as if you are on an emotional rollercoaster. If you experience this, be gentle with yourself. Do not worry. Anxiety will only agitate and amplify the new sensations you are feeling. All that is happening is your energetic spatial awareness is shifting. Don't resist, as this can make you panic, especially if you are ultra-sensitive.

Your soul is a wise, guiding intelligence that always wants what's best for you. Any negative symptoms of energy you feel have always been there. You just haven't been aware of them until now. I always say better out than in. Those hidden energies are the reason why you may be experiencing financial blockages, relationship struggles, or a non-existent love life. You've got to move them out. Meditation helps. Muster up faith, even an ounce of it, and eventually it will become a mountain of strength that will give you the ability to have a clear perspective of your life and the steps that you need to take.

Unleash the Psychic In You

IT'S TIME TO DECIDE!

"You must train your intuition—you must trust the small voice inside you which tells you exactly what to say, what to decide."
—Ingrid Bergman

De·ci·sion *(di-**sihz**-on) n. 1. a position reached after consideration 2. unwavering firmness of action, character or will.*
—Roget's II: The New Thesaurus

Intuition is especially useful in decision-making. Decisions have to be made all day long and if you don't decide for yourself, life will throw you around. A good decision is when you make a clear choice. Clear choices always lead to greater opportunities and the ultimate fruition of your desires. A bad decision is when you make no choice or a tentative choice, which is essentially the same thing as making no choice. If you fail to make decisions you will have weak boundaries and you'll likely be miserable. If you use your intuition to make decisions, the process will turn from obligation to empowerment.

Usually the more important a decision people have in front of them the longer it takes for them to make a decision. Waiting to decide is not always in their best interest. Procrastination about making decisions is a big stumbling block to living a happy and fulfilling life. Fortunately, intuition helps people make faster, more effective decisions. On the flip side, making hasty decisions without checking in with your intuition is a recipe for disaster. Fear drives the feeling both of "I'm stuck" and "I'd better act impulsively." Guidance is the answer. The key to really successful decision-making is to ask for and then follow the guidance you receive from your intuition.

Top Ten Benefits of Decision Making

Let's look at the specific benefits of making confident, clear decisions based on your intuition.

1. You create your own destiny. Of course you cannot control other people or your environment, however you can decide how you respond to people and you have a choice as to how you behave and experience your environment.

2. You are no pushover. Anyone who knows you soon comes to learn this, which means you establish relationships built on a foundation of respect.

3. You create strong emotional and energetic boundaries. People who do not respect your decisions are not worthy of your time. Even if you cannot avoid someone who ignores your boundaries, for instance because you share the same workplace, you see this clearly because you understand your decisions, so you know to keep communication to a minimum and protect your energetic boundaries. You can walk away any time you feel that your needs are not being met in a relationship.

4. You eliminate worry and stress. When you make a decision you are committing to a course of action and taking responsibility. If you do the best you can to follow through on your decision, then anxiety and stress won't have a place in your mind.

5. *Your life is more enjoyable.* When you decide, you can live more fully in the present and you are not waiting for others to take charge of your destiny. If you think you have to wait for someone else to make your choices be aware that this is a decision. If you make your own choices you can have more of what you want, and sooner.

6. *Your sense of overwhelm disappears.* When you embrace the process of decision-making you gain clarity and generate powerful momentum in your life.

7. *You have more time available to you.* Procrastination is one of the greatest time wasters. People who procrastinate spend hours debating whether they should or should not do things. When you make decisions instead of sitting on them, procrastination releases its grip on you.

8. *You won't feel the need to complain and blame.* Complaining and blaming others are history when you take responsibility for making your own decisions. Because you are self-reliant and accountable to yourself you create healthy, balanced relationships.

9. *You never have to wonder "What if?"* When you make a clear-cut decision, you don't have to wonder what might have happened. You have few regrets. You follow your intuition and back it up with necessary research, then complete your next action step.

10. *You attract more opportunities to you.* When you send an energetic message out into the universe that says, "I'm in the flow and I decide consciously," opportunities open up for you. You are not caught up in the subtle energies of fear that were previously a distraction and confused the universe about the direction you were headed.

Top Ten Reasons Why You Make Poor Decisions

Have you ever known a course of action to take and not followed through on it? Have you ever had a strong gut instinct not to do something, but gone ahead and done it anyway, and then regretted doing it? Do you often waffle and delay when you are faced with a decision? The more you ignore your intuition and the less you rely upon it, the weaker it gets.

Let's look at the top ten reasons people don't make clear decisions, so you can overcome these negative patterns and eliminate them from your life once and for all.

1. Doubt. The number one reason people get stuck is the thought, "What if I make the wrong choice?" Hello! If you don't make a decision, nothing is going to change. You can complain about your situation all you want and it won't help you a bit. I love being supportive and cheerleading my clients, however I have no time for excuses. I refuse to work with people who are not willing to take even a small risk.

If you make a decision and you miss your target, aim again. A wrong choice in truth is not wrong. Doing the best you can is all that matters. Go back to the drawing board and look at what led you to make that choice. Any type of doubt creates a distortion in reality that will influence the clarity of your decision-making.

2. Denial. When we're not honest with ourselves it spills over into all our relationships. It plays a role in people pleasing and is a mask hiding our discomfort. For instance, it's B.S.

when people say, "I haven't acted because I don't want to hurt anyone's feelings." Denial is a form of self-sabotage that has to be tackled and dealt with appropriately if people truly want to stop being paralyzed by indecision. You can save yourself time and money by being honest with yourself and others about your motivations. From the perspective of your intuition, you will see that the truth is not about the other, it's about you: "I may get hurt because I might not get what I want." When you speak with sincerity, even if you don't get the response you want, at least you've been honest about your needs. Also, that person may say, "Yes," even though you feared they'd say "No." Often stating your needs opens up a higher level of dialogue and new options appear. Don't commit to doing something if you know that you will suffer in the process. It's not necessary to compromise your needs.

3. Rejection. Several years ago I dated a strong willed man. I let myself get carried along in his life without making clear decisions that would help me establish healthy boundaries. The longer we dated, the more I let him have his own way. I was passive and weak because I feared rejection. I couldn't bear the thought of it. Guess what happened? When I spoke up for my needs, he dumped me. Because I didn't make clear decisions and follow through on my instincts about what I needed, I experienced low self-esteem and shame when that relationship came to a close.

4. Lust. There is a big difference between love and lust. Love is steady, expanding, deep, and secure. Lust is fireworks, intensity, obsession, and distraction. Love is like the depths of the ocean. When you feel a crazy high-low feeling, it's most definitely lust. I've seen many of my clients blinded by lust. It shuts down the intuition. The intensity of their emotions overrides the subtle energies of their guidance. Lust can make you lose sense of reality. It is the fastest way to fall into denial about the decisions that have to be made. Have you ever seen an infatuated person who stopped taking responsibility for all other areas of their life than his or her sexual relationship? When in lust, it's easy to ignore the bills and let goals that you are passionate about be put on the backburner. By contrast, when you are in a mutually loving relationship, you will be able to make the most challenging decisions with confidence.

5. Perfectionism. It is important to have excellent standards, however people never get anything done when their standards are unrealistically high. They talk about what they need to do. They often know what they need to do. They might even obsess over the details of attaining their goals. However, they don't follow through because they have no shot of meeting such high standards. Do you have a project, goal, or task that you want to complete and yet it's still not done? Would it be better to strive for perfection and write the "perfect book" (which isn't really ideal because it's only ten pages long and still isn't published) or would it be better to get over your ego and publish a book that will make you feel great and help others? Work on improving your standards as you go along. I like the expression "Practice makes perfect" because it encourages doing and moving forward rather than circling around an idea in your head over and over. When a thought remains longer than is necessary inside you there is no space for expanded awareness to present new opportunities and new ideas to you.

6. Fear. One of the fastest ways to bring decision making to a grinding halt is fear. It is ironic that "What ifs?" can paralyze people. When people operate from fear, you know what? That fear comes true. When people focus on possible negatives, they suggest to the unconscious mind that it bring forth a situation, environment, or people who will fulfill that vision. For instance, some of my clients are baffled that they can't find true love. But they are constantly fearful about the men they meet. They fear being alone, rejected, abandoned, used, and abused. Because their unconscious minds are fixated on fear they won't meet Mr. Right. Fear can start out very small and then grow very big within you. Therefore, as soon as you discover you have a fear, sit down and evaluate its specifics. Where does the fear come from inside your body? If your fear had an emotion, what would it be? On a scale of 1 to 10, with 1 being minimal fear and 10 being paralyzing fear, what number would you chose? Does the fear relate to a person, task, or environment? When did you first feel blocked by this fear? Dissecting your fear will stop it from having power over you. It is the unknown that triggers the most fear in people. When you educate yourself, your fears will transform into clarity and you will be presented with a gentle next step.

7. *Judgment.* Being critical of other people is a sure-fire way to disconnect from your intuition and prevent wise decision-making. The energetic action of judgment is to focus your will outside you. This makes people feel powerful and puffed up on the surface, but don't be fooled if you do this. This is a temporary feeling of well-being. Whether the person you are judging has or hasn't done something bad or wrong, it is not your responsibility to criticize their actions. When you are judgmental, you only perceive a person or situation from a negative standpoint. This separates your mind from devising solutions that could help the person or improve the situation.

Judgment is one of the toughest behaviors to temper. It takes constant practice. The more critical you are of others in your daily life, the more you will unconsciously fear being criticized. And when you fear criticism, you play it safe. The outcome is a life of mediocrity. A simple life is not mediocre, if it gives someone happiness. Not everyone is striving for the American Dream or to live in the Fairy Princess Castle. Mediocrity is compromising the integrity of the soul. How do you know when you are doing this? Your inner indicator is a physical feeling of dissatisfaction. Your outer indicator is that your environment has a grey energy that very subtly coats everything you see. Judgment is an energy zapper, and nonetheless everyone does it. If you think you never judge, you're in denial. Judgment stems from inner pain. It is a temporary and ineffective solution for making pain go away.

8. *Resentment.* Unchecked feelings can fester internally and fill people's thoughts so much that there is no space for intuition to speak to them. Most of the time resentment stems from misunderstanding. The person who holds the resentment has taken the actions of another as a personal dig or an attack. I see this most commonly in love relationships. A woman is hurt and jealous because she thinks a man did what he did on purpose. Her acute case of resentment then turns into obsession. Thoughts fill the woman's head. She needs clarity to decide on her next best step yet her resentment is blocking her ability to take care of herself and make an effective decision. Resentment is toxic and dangerous because energetically it puts walls of anger around you. It stops the love this woman wants more than anything from being able to reach her. From a clairvoyant perspective the expression, "She gave me the cold shoulder," is when a man approaches a woman in person, via email, or on the phone and her resentment creates a steel wall.

There is a huge difference between setting a healthy boundary and shutting someone out. When you act from resentment, you cut off any possibility of love. Resentment kills love and eats away inside you. Every choice you make comes from a place of weakness resulting in pain. You can kid yourself that you're in control. But the only person who suffers from your denial is you. If you have good cause to feel resentment because someone did do something hurtful instead of holding it against that person, let the person go from your life. Once the person is outside of your energetic space, the resentment will be released. It is easy to dismiss feelings and thoughts as unimportant because they are intangible. But they are real. And it is only a matter of time before they become physically manifest. Listen to your body, acknowledge your true feelings, and take care of yourself. That is a powerful decision you can make right now especially if you are feeling resentful.

9. Self-esteem. People with poor self-esteem consistently deflect making decisions. The main reason for this is that they think they don't deserve what they want and making a decision would be the first step towards them receiving it. They live in the world of Never Never Land. For instance, they wonder why ten years after starting a career they are still only earning $20 an hour. Even though they know they are worth more, they can't see how to create prosperity. Or they're still talking about the big business deal that is in the works. It's always about to happen, yet they never asked for what they wanted or took the steps to manifest the deal because their low self-esteem told them, "You don't deserve it, so don't ask." How ironic that they don't get what they want and low self esteem wins.

An important part of the decision-making process is making the active conscious choice to ask. If you don't ask, you don't get.

If your ego resists this advice, telling you that you can receive when you don't ask, I would agree. In some cases you can receive without asking. However, by not asking you're leaving things to chance. You're putting your creativity to sleep because you are deferring your choices to other people. Luck doesn't get you what you want. You need to choose to be receptive to abundance. You have to put yourself in the right situations, around the right people, and in the right environments. This can only happen when your self-esteem is elevated. Remind yourself every day, "I deserve the best of everything."

10. Blame. The second most effective block to personal power is to blame someone else. The best way to stay stuck is to blame yourself. When you blame yourself, you send a message to your unconscious mind that says, "I don't trust you." Would you give someone you don't trust your checking account pin code? After I made a series of poor decisions, I continually blamed myself. I kept going over in my head what I could have done differently. I was in, "What if," mode and it had me spinning on a wheel. Sometimes I put all the blame on my boyfriend, other times I immersed myself in self-recrimination. This kept me paralyzed, stuck in evaluating my past decisions. It stopped me from seeing a present day solution, a way to do things differently in the future. Only when I kicked blame out of my mind did clarity and opportunity flow to me. Over time I caught myself quicker and quicker whenever the blame syndrome tried to creep back in and take hold of my mind like a python. "Oh no, out you go!" I'd say. Stop blaming others and stop blaming yourself. It's a waste of energy. Learn from my mistake. You'll feel so much better when you are pro-active. It takes courage to make a decision after you've made a big mistake. But it's not a mistake if you learn from it. It's a lesson. Learning is how you develop wisdom and clarity.

Begin an Intuition Journal

I've always had a passion for writing. I find it incredibly healing. I experience writing as an alchemical process, meaning any time I have a negative feeling, get stuck in my head, or feel overwhelmed I write. You may think you know what you're thinking and feeling, however, I've discovered that denial is deceptive and hard to penetrate. A good way to overcome this problem is to write your thoughts and feelings in a journal.

A journal is a sacred space for you to be honest and not be judged. Journaling is an excellent way to defuse hurt and anger. It also creates space in your mind for new insights to be received. There are a couple of different ways you can journal. One of the techniques I use is to write like I'm speaking to my best friend. In the past, I bitched and blamed for pages and pages. Now I find myself writing pages of gratitude.

Another technique I like is writing a question to myself and allowing my pen to move across the page without thinking as I write. Then I read the answer. I'm always amazed at the wisdom on the page. I know it is coming from a higher source of wisdom that flows through me.

I remember when I broke up with my ex-fiancé. I went to a little boutique in a quaint side street of Hampstead, London, and bought myself a hardback journal with a gorgeous little fairy sitting on a mushroom. Other fairies surrounded her and all their wings were covered in glitter. Inside the journal were crisp white pages with faint reddish-brown lines on them. That helped me to write straight! I took that journal everywhere I went and wrote. I wrote on the subway, I wrote waiting for friends, and I wrote before going on the air when I did the TV show. Writing healed my heart and continues to do so.

I recommend buying yourself a journal that makes you feel special. How I am feeling determines the type of journal I choose. Right now, I am using a softbound, letter size pad that has a black cover. Over the years, I've written approximately twenty journals. Earlier this year, when I returned to Los Angeles after a trip to the UK, before writing this book, I burned every single one of them in my garden. You may wonder why I did this. I knew my past thoughts were energetically held in the pages. I knew I needed to let go of everything I'd written in the past to be able to write this book from my heart.

I encourage you to give journaling a chance. Begin by writing your thoughts and feelings when you need to gain some clarity, or try using the following two exercises to overcome the common decision-making obstacle of perfectionism and to neutralize the voice of the inner critic. You can download FREE journal pages at: **www.AmericansIntuitionCoach.com/journal**.

Journal Exercise #1: Technique for Curing Perfectionism

Pick an overdue goal, project, or task that has to get done. Note in your intuition journal when you have decided to complete it. Every time you don't follow through on a commitment that would move you towards this goal because you are concerned that you won't do it well enough, write down three things in your journal:

- The time and date of when perfectionism got in your way

- How it made you feel

- Why you felt stuck

You may think the reasons for your perfectionism are obvious. However, if so, why haven't you bypassed them and taken action? The energies that hold you back are subtle and complex, so when you leave this limiting pattern room to grow the toll it takes on you increases. There may be times when you think you are overreacting to a negative pattern of perfectionism or you'll rationalize it, "Oh, it's not that bad." So why do you feel frustrated and drained around the issue of this project? Why when you go to take action does exhaustion sweep over you and make you want to take a quick nap before doing what you know you need to do?

Don't skip writing down your experience and don't skip reading what you wrote. When you see it written on the page, the hidden subtle energies blocking you will move into your conscious awareness. You may tell yourself, "It's a waste of time," or "This is stupid," and you may ask, "How is writing it down going to make any difference?" On the page, your thought looks different from when it is inside your head.

I recommend an additional step if you are serious about moving through your block. Share what you have written with someone you can trust. If you can't think of anyone you can open up to and trust, check out a non-profit group called Al-Anon. When you allow someone to bear witness to what you have written and when you speak it aloud to another human being, a powerful transformation occurs. Truth begins to override your denial about your behavior. If you do this exercise only half-assed, you are going to get mediocre results. You have everything to gain and nothing to lose. The worst thing that could happen here is that your block remains. No change. The best thing that could occur is that you complete your goal and build your confidence and self-esteem.

Journal Exercise #2: Neutralizing the Inner Critic

Your inner critic will stop you in your tracks every time you come up with an idea that moves you closer to your heart's desire if you don't acknowledge its voice. The more you ignore it, the louder it will get. So take ten minutes at the end of your day to write down all the people and situations that bothered you. Don't hold back. Get every single criticism down on the page where it can be acknowledged.

If you want to take this a step further because you feel ready to purge your inner critic then read back what you wrote aloud and record it. Schedule a time to listen to the recording 48 hours later. Make sure this will be uninterrupted time. Listen to all of what you wrote. This is a particularly effective exercise if you are going through a power struggle in a relationship. You can create a profound healing for yourself by using it. At the time, you may not be aware of the transformation. However you will soon see the positive effects if you stick with it on a daily basis. Afterwards you'll make new decisions from a pure, heartfelt connection. When you do, it's a win-win for everyone.

The Fuel of Indecision

Undefined boundaries with others are a catalyst for indecision. Some people complain that they feel imposed upon or disrespected in their relationships. When I investigated further with a client who had this problem, it turned out she had never considered her own needs or expressed them. No wonder people were walking all over her and she felt pain. Once she had conscious awareness that she could delineate boundaries, she became afraid. She didn't know what the consequences of stating her needs would be. She feared change. She didn't feel she had the right to choose how people would treat her. She thought her circumstances happened to her and that she had no control over life.

This idea had been keeping her stuck for years. She'd become so used to feeling trapped that the possibility of making a decision was daunting. Instead of feeling regret and remorse and then falling into denial, I encouraged her to look in detail at her past to identify circumstances that had triggered indecision in her life. It usually had to do with her fear of rocking the boat. We saw that behind this indecision actually was great clarity. She knew what she wanted. Thankfully she was willing to reclaim her hidden treasure. We created a plan for her to be more vigilant of her moments of indecision.

It is easy to fall into the "I'll deal with it later" mentality. If this happens to you it's because you don't want to feel discomfort in your body or mind. When someone isn't aware of having uncomfortable feelings, they get off the basketball court of life and go to the sidelines. It seems like an easier choice. But it's not. When you've been on the bench for a while, it's harder to get back in the game with the people who have been constantly practicing on the court. The uneasier you feel in your body, the greater an indication it is that a past issue regarding your identity is coming to the surface.

If you could use a plastic bag or a Chanel handbag, what would you choose? That Chanel handbag is your intuition. It is the key to your creativity. You can let go of your fear of change when you trust your intuition. Transition can be scary when you can't see what lies ahead of you.

I'm inspired by Napoleon Hill's philosophy in *Think and Grow Rich* when he speaks of the need to burn one's bridges to create powerful transformation. It is important to understand when to transition and when to burn your bridges in regard to career and relationships. That's where intuition comes in handy.

When the movie *The Secret* was released, I had clients say to me, "I watched *The Secret* and it's not working. I got rid of all the types of things in my life that I didn't want to attract and now I'm out of a job and my husband is pissed." The law of attraction that *The Secret* teaches is absolutely rewarding for people who apply its principles religiously. People who criticize *The Secret* perceive it as advice to use the universe as an ATM. Pop in a four-digit code, hit enter, and, yippee, you get a new house, a new soul mate, and new multi-millionaire status. However, the universe is not an ATM. The law of attraction doesn't work when you're passive. You have to learn the art of balance, which is being in the flow of the universe. The more you apply the law of attraction in your life the easier it will be to delineate when to be moved along by the vibrational current of attraction that you have chosen and when to be proactive. That's why this chapter is all about decision.

So if you poo-poo'd *The Secret* and think it's baloney, pick the DVD back up and watch it five days in a row. Schedule it in Monday through Friday. No excuses! If something hasn't manifested yet in your life that you want, it's because you haven't fully chosen it and you're not taking all the necessary steps.

Another factor to consider is that you live in the third dimension and there are universal laws that determine how fast goals and ideas come to fruition. George Lucas may have wanted to make *Star Wars* in twenty-four hours, however this would have been impossible because of how our time-space reality operates. Universal laws are there for a reason. That reason is to keep our world in balance. There are nine months of pregnancy to allow a human to integrate the forthcoming change.

We like to think we understand nature but we don't really. Only people who live in pristine nature 24/7 are attuned. They are the most intuitive. Often we are moving against the energy of creation. We are trying to force it to change and it won't. With our consistent force, we may create destruction. Destruction is creation in reverse.

In truth, we are always making choices even when we don't make a proactive decision. When we don't have an answer of what to do, it's because we are choosing to be ignorant. We're unwilling to take the time to learn.

You have the opportunity to create an amazing life. Why settle for mediocre? All you have to do is choose.

Recognizing the Voice of Intuition

When you make a choice, energy flows to you rapidly. This is why some people get overwhelmed when presented with a decision. From an energetic perspective, the bigger the decision, the more impact it will have. More energy is present, so greater focus and awareness is required to ensure that you stay on target with your goals.

Imagine you decide to begin your own business. You've always wanted to have your own company so you can have lots of money, no boss telling you what to do, and the luxury of choosing how you work and when you work. Except from the beginning it isn't working out how you wanted. You're six months into business development and there seems to be no light at the end of the tunnel. All your original motivations for setting up the business have not come to fruition. In fact things have gotten worse. There's no guaranteed weekly paycheck, no guidance from a manager or boss to support you, and no structure to your day. Your business is fly by the seat of your pants, chaotic. Any ounce of creativity you had is being zapped. You are wondering why you ever thought this was a good idea.

If you feel like you're on a sinking ship, you need access to your intuition more than ever. At this point, it may feel like a hundred different voices are speaking in your head and telling you to do different things. Your first step now is to make a clear plan. Realize that planning and structuring your business in advance of its set up or even in the midst of working will be integral to its survival. Winging it is like playing Russian roulette. Yes, you could survive without planning, but why put yourself through so much stress? The more specific the choices you make in advance, the better prepared you will be. Add your intuition into your decision-making process as you set up this plan.

Using your intuition will take you a quantum leap beyond where you are aiming. Have you ever had an idea or goal and it's turned out better than you expected? This is intuition at work, acting as your coach while you play ball on the court. To hear your intuition you have to stop and get quiet. You have to take occasional timeouts. A timeout in basketball is not a stop. It's a strategic pause in action that gives the players (yes, that's you) an opportunity to connect with and receive guidance from the coach. In your case, your coach is your higher self or your spirit guides. Once players have integrated the guidance, they have the opportunity to make amazing shots because everyone is in synch.

The player who is in his head while the coach is speaking to him will miss the benefits of intuitive guidance. Your practice is to apply strategy that comes from within the expansiveness of intuition. Combining the skills of intuition and decision-making will make you formidable. You're not going to get your business right over night. You're going to have wins and losses. However there are plenty of games to play in every season. If you keep persisting, you can make it to the playoffs. Once in the playoffs, the stakes will be raised but the level of your play will be higher, as you'll be working with consistent energy patterns that are stronger.

I am an LA Lakers fan. In 2008, in order to win the Western Conference Championship, the Lakers were scheduled to play Denver for seven games in the first round of the playoffs. They had to master the Denver Nuggets' energy patterns if they wanted to defeat them and move to the next level in four games instead of seven. The faster you master the energy patterns of your business the faster you'll move, too. Basically, energy is constantly transforming and your intuition will help you to make smooth transitions. You can't be complacent. You have to constantly adapt.

There is this misconception that you become psychic and suddenly you know everything. That would be complete God realization. That's a lifelong goal at best. In fact the way I understand it is that it's an eternal state of being. When resisting change, it makes it hard to get to the next level.

If the Lakers had played the same strategy in the next round against the San Antonio Spurs as they had against Denver, it could have lost them the game. They knew they had to adapt. Like them, you need to adapt. At first it can feel awkward when you are doing things differently, however if you keep charging forward, you'll feel a sudden click inside and your intuition will guide you. Instead of stumbling you'll begin striding. This will move you beyond obstacles that may have held you back in the past. They won't even be on your radar now. If in the process of doing business you start hearing a voice of fear in your head, take the time out. It will be worth it.

So how do you recognize the voice of fear? Well, for starters, notice that when things are getting worse and you are getting more agitated, worried, and frustrated, fear is in your driver's seat. By contrast, you'll know your intuition is leading you when despite surrounding chaos or seemingly insurmountable problems you feel unusually calm and centered. Follow your intuition even if people around you think you are losing it and making bad decisions and they criticize you. Have you ever been in a crisis and a faint voice within has said, "Everything will be all right," and it was? That's intuition.

The voice of fear sometimes wants you to make hasty decisions. The voice of intuition gives you steps to take. Sometimes it is only one step at a time and following this step takes courage. Your reward will be that you are cloaked in faith. Faith leads to peace. This is a great feeling and one you deserve to experience more often.

Have you ever had the experience of dating someone who was not a good match for you, sharing what happened with friends six months later, and had them say, "Told you so" or "I already knew that?" When I told my friends I'd split from my fiancé, they confessed, "I didn't trust him" and "Finally! He was bad news for you."

"Why didn't you tell me?" I asked.

Their answers were: "Didn't want to upset you," "Wanted to see you happy and if that was what you wanted…"

Yes, the psychic was last to realize she was in a crappy relationship that smelt like wilted and rotting two-week-old roses. The funny thing is that I still did great psychic readings during that time period.

How could I receive clear guidance for others and yet be blind when it came to my own life? There are a few reasons why I couldn't see the truth of my situation. First, I had old wounds, mostly emotional, which were trapped in my unconscious mind and in my body at a cellular level. A wound can be experienced in one of your four predominant bodies: physical, emotional, mental, and spiritual, or in all of them at once. Even though I could tap into the universal super-conscious mind and access my sixth sense on behalf of my clients, that access was denied me when I wanted something for myself because it was triggering past wounds that were unresolved.

The way to determine you have an unconscious block is if you're trying to make a situation or relationship in your life work harmoniously and you feel resistance in your body, this is an indicator that you have a block.

My desire to be in a loving relationship was so intense that any warning signs my intuition gave me fell on deaf ears. I was only focused on experiencing perfect love. I remember being really into this guy and telling my friends how he said he loved me, but I wondered why he wouldn't commit to our relationship and why he was sleeping with someone else.

My dad could see the truth. He said, "Joanna, you're walking around with a neon sign on your head that says, 'I'm an idiot. Screw me.'" At the time I was most offended. How could Dad say something like this to his daughter? But he was right. He'd seen me turn this neon sign on and off for many years and he'd seen enough. It took me a long time to understand that I was the one creating my own problem.

If you keep attracting the wrong partners who don't fit into your "Happily Ever After" relationship dreams and you keep crashing and burning every time there's new love, face it, you've got a blind spot just like I did. A part of me enjoyed being stuck because this created drama in my life, I got the attention I craved, it was a distraction that enabled me to ignore my untended wounds, and I didn't have to change.

Can you relate to any of my past blocks? If you're stuck in an area of your life but you can't relate, then you most certainly have a blind spot. If your life is perfect with no challenges, wow, congratulations.

I am the eternal student. Since those days I've learned that keeping myself in the dark is painful. The person who suffered most from not addressing my wounds was I. Now when I sense I have a blind spot, I face it head on. If I can't easily gain clarity, I'll do a couple of different techniques to get to the root of the problem.

There are many techniques for uncovering the truth that's at the root of your blind spots, which I've put together as easy-to-follow exercises in my Intuition Development System. You can find out more at: **www.IntuitionDevelopmentSystem.com**.

If something isn't going the way I want and I can't see why, I'll clear the decks for an hour in the middle of the day to meditate. You may protest, "There's no way I can stop working in the middle of the day" or "I have too much on my plate." I understand, believe me! The thing is, if you don't stop, the problem won't go away. This small problem will slowly grow until one day it's so big that you'll go through the small internal door of your unconscious mind and exclaim, "How the hell did this elephant get in here?"

Once a blind spot has grown into a full-size elephant, it's a momentous task to get it out of your space. Of course it can be removed, however it takes a lot longer. It's like putting off going to the dentist. If you don't go for two years, chances are you're going to get fillings when you do eventually go. So my suggestion is take action now.

Blind Spot Removal Exercise

Find somewhere quiet to sit or lie down comfortably to ensure that your focus is not upon discomfort in your body. Then close your eyes and take several deep breaths into your body. Now call upon your guardian angel or spirit guides. Don't worry if you feel like you are making this up, just go with it.

I pray directly to God, as that's what works for me. Practice using your intuition and see what works best for you. In the past, I've called upon one guide and sometimes another one has appeared for support because this different guide would be more helpful for the problem I was asking about. I also want to clarify that when I pray to God, I am not focused on a deity from any specific religion.

With eyes closed, I say, "I call for the best guidance possible to help me see my blind spot clearly, and I ask that a solution be presented to me." Then I go on to express the specific situations that are troubling me. I then allow myself to receive guidance.

The size of the elephant in your subconscious mind will be a determining factor as to how fast you receive clarity. The answer can come immediately or it can take longer.

When I was working in production at MTV I had a lot of good times, however my soul felt undernourished. The voice of my intuition began telling me that it was time to quit my job and move out of my comfort zone. All sorts of questions arose: "When should I leave? What shall I do? How will I make money? Will I regret my decision? Because of my past mistakes, how do I know I can really trust the inner guidance I am receiving?"

Here's how I handled my uncertainty. First, I'd pop out of the office for ten minutes and go find a quiet bench to sit on and connect inwards. That helped me get perspective on my situation. That got me out of everyone else's drama and the spin that they were experiencing. It helped me to stop absorbing it.

Second, at the end of my fifteen-hour day, I'd meditate right before going to sleep. I'd close my eyes with intention in the hope that my blindness would be revealed to me and I'd say, "Dear God, please show me what is the best next step for me to take? Is it for my highest good to keep working at MTV?" Then I'd let go of my question and fall asleep. In the morning, I'd hear a voice inside my head say, "It is time to leave MTV."

At this point, I was only halfway through the season on a show and it still had several months to go so leaving didn't seem like a responsible thing to abandon ship. Of course, I wanted to make sure I wasn't projecting my desire to move on from this job into my own head and sabotage myself by being impulsive. But I felt confirmation of the message in my body. Every time I walked into the MTV offices in Santa Monica I could feel my stomach turn and prickles of energy hitting my aura. The MTV office was a great environment to work in, but I could feel it wasn't right for me anymore.

Every night for thirty days, I'd ask the same question before going to sleep. This meant I wasn't just falling asleep. I was entering sleep with the intention of meditation and being open to higher guidance. It gave a message to my unconscious to release my limiting beliefs. Every morning, I received the same message, "Leave MTV." After the thirty days, I handed my notice in and it felt like a weight had been lifted from me.

Taking thirty days to ask before acting confirmed to me that the lesson I needed to learn in that environment was complete and it was time for me to move on. What I would be moving on to was unknown. This meant that I had to have faith. If I truly wanted to help people understand how to awaken their intuition, it was time for me to commit to it.

After I left MTV on good terms, I was invited back to do other shoots. A part of me wanted to do them, because I love TV production and had made great friendships while I was there, but I declined. My inner guidance told me, "Stay focused on your next step." That step was to write this book that you are now reading.

Accountability

If you are committed to developing your intuition, you can overcome even the most paralyzing self-doubt. The first step is faith. Without it, you're not going to be able to access intuitive guidance. How do you activate faith if you have none? You stop doing things how you have been doing them. Whatever you've been doing up to this point hasn't worked for you. Instead, sit in the energy of not-doing and not-knowing.

This is going to feel pretty uncomfortable. You'll definitely want to do something to take your mind off of how you're feeling. But stand firm. Be strong. The discomfort will pass. It's likely you will get triggered in your solar plexus, which is the area just above your navel. The sensations of being triggered can feel like you are dropping on a roller coaster, or pancakes being flipped in your tummy, a sharp shooting pain, or pure nausea. I've had all three of those triggers at once. If you have, too, you already know it's pretty intense. However, it's a good sign, because it means the sabotaging self-doubt that usually plays havoc in your life is now being squeezed to the surface.

Self-doubt doesn't like to be the center of attention. It likes to be the one pointing the finger here there and everywhere without having to do anything itself. Don't let it run your life or you'll have so many regrets and disappointments of "what could have been."

Your second step is to ignore the voice of your ego, which is actually what self-doubt is. Ego doesn't want to risk looking bad. Ego thinks it's better to maintain the status quo. Ego fears change. Your ego will do it's best to instill fear in you, and if it gets its way it'll manifest as multiple doubts in your life.

Do you have any projects that you started with excitement and yet they're still not anywhere near being done? Self-doubt leads to procrastination, which leads to frustration, which leads to being stuck.

When self-doubt takes hold, take this third step. Give yourself a little pep talk, like one you would give to a dear friend. You could model one of my past pep talks I've given to myself: "The fear I'm feeling is irrational. It is because of an old wound. That wound is in the past. Doubt, you have no power over me and there is no room for you in my life. Goodbye. I have faith in myself. I'm doing the best I can. I'm open to seeing new ways of approaching this situation. Give me a first step and I promise to do it."

The fourth and final step is set a time and date to do what you promised to do. Without a concrete commitment, you'll revert to self-doubt. You're highly likely to self-sabotage so write down the time and date, and share this information with a friend you can trust to hold you accountable.

I've seen so many people renege on promises. I've done it myself. As human beings, we don't mean to, but we do when the energy of self-doubt is big inside our minds. Check in with yourself and ask: "Will I remain accountable?" If there's an ounce of doubt present you've got to raise your accountability stakes.

When I was in a writing group, the way I ensured that I would get a chapter of my book written one week was to promise that I'd give each person in the group $100 if I didn't get it done when I said I would. Did I write the chapter? Absolutely.

Have you ever experienced everything going your way? You thought to yourself, "This is too good to be true," and then you hit the wall? Perhaps your relationship started going downhill, your finances dried up, you developed health concerns, or you had so much work on your plate that you couldn't move ahead. What has happened is that you got used to being surrounded by a glob of energy and so you avoided addressing it. Originally it didn't seem so bad, and then it grew a little more and a little more.

The way you could experience this kind of energy in your life is debt. You're $1,000 overdrawn and before you've had time to assimilate this you're at $10,000, then one day you're $50,000 in the red and it looks like it happened to you, that you've had no part in it. You may rationalize the tough economy or the price increase in gas being responsible for your financial status, or like me, blame someone like my ex for a long time. But you're not facing the fact that it was you who ignored the glob of energy.

More and more often I'm hearing people say, "Oh well, my problem is that Mercury is in retrograde." Mercury Retrograde seems to be catching blame for everything now. Mercury is a planet that causes breakdowns in communication when it goes backwards in relation to the Earth's orbit. Supposedly it's responsible for breakups, computer glitches, and dropped cell phone calls. I don't buy it. I say get over this lame excuse. Astrology doesn't control your life. It is a wonderful tool to support your spiritual development. But the way the planets and stars align and your astrological sign do not mean everything is set in stone. Astrology is only a guideline.

Would you give up your dream of being a pianist if someone told you that Aquarians are natural guitar players and your sign is Aquarius? Hopefully not.

Look at it from this perspective. Let's say you're walking down a street and it is raining and you don't want to get wet, but you need to get to an audition for your dream role. You don't just say, "Oh, it raining, I'm not going to show up." Life goes on. If you're that worried about the weather check weather.com beforehand and be prepared with an umbrella. Another person will show up regardless of the rain and channel their energy into giving a great performance. It didn't matter that their hair isn't perfect. The casting director can see beyond their appearance so they will book the role.

The person who lets the rain or Mercury retrograde affect him or her stays stuck. If that's you, stop letting life happen to you. You may think you're proactive in creating the life you want because you eat, sleep, see friends, work, and make plans, but I want you to ask yourself honestly, "Am I existing or am I living a full life?"

You can develop your skill of clairvoyance (more details will be provided on this in chapter 6) to recognize your problems before they manifest into your life. Breaking a challenge down to the pure physics of its energy allows you to see what you are dealing with and to remove energy from your field that isn't working for you. Energy is energy without all the distortions we put on top of a situation. Here's how to do it.

When you have a problem, focus on the energetic space between your energy and your experience of what's going on. Imagine the problem experience as a glob of energy. Can you get a visual image of that? Can you picture the energy's size and color? Once you can see it, visualize your physical energy. Picture your physical energy merging with the energy of the problem. Then compare the two energies in size, color, tone, density, and frequency, and evaluate the imbalances between the two.

Next, clear the image of the problem energy in your mind's eye and imagine your goal as pure energy. Note its appearance and feel. Then merge your physical energy with the energy of the goal. Again look for compatibility and look for a mismatch of energy.

This exercise will help you to ascertain if you're limiting yourself, how big your block is, how far away you truly are from manifesting your goal, how aligned you are to your vision, and to evaluate if you want what you think you want, or if you now want to upgrade to a bigger goal or let it go. This is the key that can unlock your treasure chest.

Having the ability to see energy is not enough. You have to be willing to do something once you look at it. Everyone has free will. This is your life, so you decide. We humans make life complicated for ourselves. There's always a straight track, but we have the tendency to get caught up in pretty patterns that tie us in knots. Take the path of least resistance. You are not stuck. If you feel stuck, it's only that you think you are. Any successful entrepreneur will nod their head in agreement with this statement.

Be attentive to the naysayer in your mind. Stay separate from it. That energy will paralyze you if you take it on. You can choose to see, hear, and feel whatever you want. It may take you a while to grasp this. In fact, it could take your entire life. But when you understand this choice, any resistance you have will fall away and you'll experience a deep feeling of peace. I've had moments and spells of peaceful experience. I'm still learning how to feel it 24/7.

Using your intuition to evaluate opportunities through the visual skill of clairvoyance helps you to see beyond the limitations of language. We can communicate only so much through words. Have you ever been in a foreign country where you don't speak the language? Suddenly getting directions or ordering a glass of water becomes pretty difficult. You start pointing your hands or you try to look thirsty by sticking your tongue out, feeling silly in the process. Using symbolism helps us to bridge the gap to communicate our needs. This is why spirit guides give psychics information in symbols.

Use this exercise as a way to gain information to help you move beyond your blocks. Anyone can do it, all you have to do is be willing to look at your energy field and expand your perception of what you see.

The best way to strengthen your intuition is to dive right in and use it. At first it may feel awkward and challenging to approach your decision-making processes in a new way. If you have faith and keep moving forward despite any discomfort you feel, your courage will be rewarded with the answers and guidance you've been searching for.

One of the biggest fears I hear from people who want to develop their intuition is "How can I trust the guidance I'm receiving? What if it's wrong?" That's a risk you've got to be willing to take if you truly want to strengthen your intuitive muscles. Start off looking at energy with small decisions and take your time. Making hasty decisions when you're learning to trust the information you receive will set you back.

I cannot stress enough how important it is to keep yourself as centered and grounded as possible when learning how to recognize the difference between wise guidance and the voice of your ego, which will try to make you take fear-based action.

One way you can test if an answer you get using energy work is right for you is by developing the skill of *claircognizance*. This is pure knowing. The knowing is in every cell of your being. It will feel like the knowing is emanating from deep inside your body. When knowing meets any external objections, it is transparent to doubt. This enables you not to be affected or swayed by the thoughts of another person.

You may trust your answer by closely observing your physical reactions to people and situations. Each physical symptom has a different meaning. Your body is an intuition map that will constantly give you signs about your next best step. If you feel bad, if you feel uneasy, there's a reason for this. For example, I was recently working with someone who I liked immensely, however my intuition kept telling me with physical signs that this wasn't the best working relationship for this person or me. It was a good call.

If I have an important decision to make, I'll wait for several days to be sure that I'm receiving correct guidance, as I know that my personal emotions can get in the way and distort perception. Every day, I kept hearing the same answer, "Let this person go." The trouble was that I really liked this person. The longer I left making the decision I needed to make, the more intense the energy got. I felt it in my body like a tight, constricted, and uneasy sensation around my ankle. It confirmed to me that I needed to follow through on what I was hearing. I heard the same message of guidance more and more, louder and louder through increasing physical discomfort. As soon as I made the decision to let go, it was like a ball and chain had been released from my ankle. I experienced the sensation of shooting quickly to the surface of a pool and being able to breathe more easily.

Tuning into your physical sensations is just one of many ways that you can feel energy to help you determine if your internal guidance is correct. Until you are confident in your decision-making process, it's better to feel a little more discomfort for a few days, rather than make a choice that you will later regret. But when you do decide, trust it.

If you are going through rapid personal growth and spiritual transformation it can be wise to wait several days before following guidance for another good reason: Even if you're feeling 100 percent sure about what you need to do, a better opportunity may be coming down the 'pike. If you act too soon, you'll miss the option for the type of accelerated growth that's known as a quantum leap in consciousness.

A surefire way to have confidence in the guidance you receive is to develop a strong sense of the subtle energy patterns that exist in your body. This comes from practice. Our spirit is electrical in nature and as you develop sensitivity to the impulses and waves of energy that not only move through you but also are you, understanding that is experienced as deep knowing will occur for you. This takes practice, because the essence of you is multi-dimensional in nature, meaning you have layer upon layer of knowledge to access within you. With each new layer of understanding you add on, your experience will become more resonant with your highest goals.

At first, before you feel clarity, you may feel confused. But once you have clarity, even when things seem chaotic, you will feel clear even in the midst of craziness. This awareness keeps you from being stuck and moves you quicker than you can imagine towards your goals. This is true higher guidance.

Right Timing

A crucial factor to making good decisions is right timing. This is why it is beneficial for you to get into the habit of trusting your intuition. In *Goldilocks and the Three Bears*, Goldilocks goes through the process of eating porridge that's too hot and too cold before she eat porridge that's just the right temperature. She also lies in a bed that is too big and a bed that is too small before she settles into the bed that is perfect. The message of this story is analogous to time.

The timing of your decision can make guidance positive or negative depending on the situation. Constant change makes life challenging. You have to use your intuition to know when to be flexible and when to stand firm. You need to know when to do nothing and when to take action. Businesses that stay on their toes and recognize when to change are always the ones to survive rough times.

This advice doesn't mean you should be flighty and uncommitted. A strong intuition will help you see when you are slipping and taking a wrong path. If you are receptive and willing, you can quickly get back on track.

Right timing is being spontaneous instead of impulsive. It means looking at your situation from every conceivable angle and when you can't see any new angles, feel, feel, feel for the timing. Use your body as an indicator for you to take necessary action for the results you want in your life.

With practice you can attune your body to the cycles of nature. Acknowledging signs in nature will allow you to conserve your energy and use it wisely. When you become aware of your cycles of existence, huge reserves of energy are available to you that will support all the decisions you make. The feeling of resistance, like you are swimming upstream, will disappear and it will be replaced by what you'll experience as being carried along by the current of a river. Or if you're planning to achieve big goals, you'll feel like you're surfing on a big ocean wave. The way to ensure perfect timing is to stay focused on the vibration of this energy flow.

Don't think about how fast your results are coming otherwise you'll throw yourself out of the flow of the energy. Your ego will kick in and block you from your ability to make right decisions. You have to stay on top of and in front of the wave. When you learn to master this skill of riding energy waves, you will have the opportunity to create amazing results faster. Master marketer Dan Kennedy calls this experience, whereby you can achieve in twelve months what in the past may have taken you twelve years to achieve, "the Phenomenon."

The surfer who waits patiently in the ocean has faith that his perfect wave shall come. Just because you're waiting, doesn't mean nothing is happening. It's all happening. You'll see.

Chapter 4

"BLIND VISION":
You Have All the Answers, So Why Can't You See Your Blocks and Limitations?

"Visionary people are visionary partly because of the very great many things they don't see." —Berkeley Rice

Being psychic will not give you all the answers. There are additional skills you need to use in conjunction with your intuition that will show you all you need to see. If you keep looking for answers in one place and you can't find the solution, it's because you're limiting your vision. You always have the right answer inside of you.

I meet many sensitive people with natural psychic ability that struggle with their intuition. They do not know yet how to use it in their own lives. Their sixth sense ends up confusing and overwhelming them instead of giving them peace of mind because they do not understand the science and machinations of intuition. People who are challenged by sensitivity often unknowingly shut themselves off from helpful information. They are increasingly frustrated when intense emotions they want to get rid of do not go away.

I have always been incredibly sensitive to energy. I can feel people's true emotions even if they do not know how they are feeling. I can sense people's blind spots. I can sense their denial and feel their pain. I can see what they refuse to look at.

People do not consciously dismiss the truth. It's just that when the nervous system experiences shock or pain it relegates the intense feelings to the unconscious mind. The thing is, these emotions and past beliefs are still operating their lives, even if they don't believe this to be so.

When people say to me, "I can't believe my husband cheated on me" or "I was walked all over in my job, but my boss seemed so nice when I met her," on an energetic level the truth is as clear as day that the husband is unfaithful and the boss is arrogant. There are no surprises. They are dismissing the guidance of intuition. We see what we want to see and we believe what we want to believe. The reason we don't see upon occasion is that the soul knows if we look in the cold light of day it could hurt a lot.

You may be frightened to step outside of your comfort zone. Why rock the boat? So you may decide, "Everything's okay." I want your life to be more than okay. I know you can have an amazing life 24/7. You need to stop looking at what others are doing around you. Don't settle. Power and strength that are developed from within you will give you the best feeling you ever had.

Pursuing a dream is not about the size of your goal. You don't have to aim to achieve Oprah's success or run a billion-dollar business. All you need do is to live from the truth of the desires, dreams, and goals of your own soul. And the only way to do this is to pull back the velvet curtain and go backstage. Take a look at how things are running behind your scene. You may not like what you see. Or you may wish you'd done this sooner. What I know for sure is that you'll make improvements in every area of your life and past wounds will heal, even if you've been ignoring them until now.

Addressing Denial

Fear creates our blind spots. In my own life, for a long time I couldn't understand how I had razor sharp clarity about someone else's life and when it came to my own life I was stumped. Sometimes I whined, other times I blamed. Occasionally, I checked out. I was living, but at a superficial level. I fell in love with bad boys who were unavailable emotionally. This is a common blind spot. I've often heard my clients say, "Why did this man pursue me like crazy and then dump me as soon as I opened my heart?"

As gently as possible I tell them, "He was always going to move on. He was never serious about you. How could he be? From day one, he was unavailable and if you had allowed your intuition to guide you fully, you would have seen he wasn't right for you. This doesn't mean he's a bad guy. He's got major blind spots that perfectly match your blind spots. This type of man is usually incredibly sensitive. He's not a bastard out to hurt you. The truth is he's not ready to see the truth, and neither are you, and that's why you picked each other. Because he chased you doesn't mean you didn't pick him. You did."

Signs are always present. If you review in detail what happened in a past relationship that ended badly you will always find the signs. Always. Go back to the first time you met that person and write down what happened. In fact, if you do this with all your relationships you'll see a pattern emerge on the page. One of my former patterns was that I was constantly chasing bad boys, so I kept attracting charismatic bad boys.

I kidded myself for a long time. Back in 1990, the first time I met my ex-fiancé, the writing was on the wall. So how did I fall into a black hole with him?

That day I was hanging out with my best friend, Dani Behr, a TV host, at a great coffee shop called Bar Italia in Soho, London. It was 2 A.M. Here we were, two seventeen year-olds, dressed in skimpy skirts, cut-off tops, and high-heeled boots. We were ordering hot chocolate and tomato, mozzarella, and basil panini when my ex-fiancé approached us. He flirted with Dani and she wisely ignored him. He tried a couple more times, as we ate, and I felt sorry for him. When he asked about Dani, I engaged in the conversation out of politeness. He told me how hot he thought Dani was and how much he'd love to date her, and then said, "You're a nice girl."

Well we all know what happens to nice girls, right? For those of you who don't, they get trodden on. My ex-fiancé used to phone me every week to get on the guest list for the London clubs cool at that time, places like Subterranea, Iceni, and Hanover Grand. He'd make small talk and then say, "Could you put me on the list, plus four?" He irritated me, but I also felt sorry for him, so I put him on the list.

Fast-forward a couple more years. He'd still ask about Dani, but now he also hit on me. I declined, yet agreed to be friends. We'd go for coffee and chat and I made it very clear I would never date him. But obviously I reversed that decision later. I now see that from our first meeting in Bar Italia I had created an unconsciousness mindset. "My best friend is hot and I'm nice, but not hot." My low self-esteem around this guy opened the door to me ultimately beginning a relationship with him. If you'd seen us hanging out together, you would have thought I was self-assured and confident. I'd tricked myself into believing that I was. In truth, I was immensely insecure and that impaired my ability to make wise choices.

Leap forward again in time to 2003. I'd allowed myself to evolve more and more denial that created blind spot upon blind spot about this man and our relationship until I was entirely in the dark. I was so invested in the relationship that I feared if I walked away I'd lose everything. The repercussions were that I was unable to trust my intuition and my biggest fears became my reality.

Emotions that can create blind spots include low self-esteem, anger, jealousy, resentment, frustration, and lust. The key to developing strong intuition and removing blind spots is clearing the energy in your aura, your electromagnetic field, and every cell of your being at a physical, emotional, mental and spiritual vibrational frequency. Your aura is an extension of your energy that is subtle in appearance compared to your physical body's energy. It emanates as a luminous light approximately an inch to a foot thick around the body depending on how closed or open you are. Your electromagnetic field is a combination of electrical and magnetic particles of energy that extend out in waves or lines of energy beyond your physical form depending on your thoughts and emotions. Introspection has to be at every level because these types of energy, which are beyond your conscious awareness, influence everything you want to create.

If you commit to the process of clearing your aura and you are consistent in this practice, you'll remove blocks and stagnant energy from your life. The speed at which you get the results you want depends on how much energy there is to clear. The skill of clairvoyance, which is the ability to see energy, comes in handy for evaluating the necessary level of damage control. Once your clairvoyance develops you can gain a clear picture of the amount of time and effort you need to commit to any problem at hand.

Be aware that you can never be too clairvoyant or too sensitive. The positive aspects of these qualities in their highest manifestation are absolute truth and total connectedness. The reason most people don't allow themselves to live in 100 percent truth is that truth is absolute power, and power scares them. Because only a few people live in this way, there is a misconception that it is easier to remain unconscious.

When you feel the powerful energy of truth running through you it comes with a big responsibility. Once you are awake, there's no going back to sleep again. Once the light shines on your unconscious, you may never be unconscious in this area of knowing again. You may ignore or deny the knowing. But if you do, it creates internal suffering. Remember that pain is an indication of self-deception.

As you are becoming more adept in recognizing your blind spots, you may experience turbulent emotions. You'll be calm and serene one moment, depressed and overwhelmed the next. Don't worry. This is a normal phase of intuitive development.

By the way, professional psychics have as much trouble handling the truth as anyone else. They can be devilish and manipulative at times. A misconception is that we are like Buddha and angels. I've met a few good psychics who need to have their mouths washed out with soap and water. When I was first getting into the psychic world I thought I was holier than thou. I went around saying how mean, rude, and competitive those psychics were, however I was no different than them when I perceived them that way. I was unknowingly manipulative. I thought that I knew what was best for everyone else. If you ever feel that way, your blocked emotions are getting in your way.

There is a big responsibility to give supportive guidance when giving a psychic reading and that's a lot of responsibility. Do yourself a favor and develop your intuition but don't fall into the trap of trying to fix people or push your opinions on them.

This is not a test. You can't fail. It's an exciting journey. I've had many rewarding revelations along the way as I've embraced my intuition. Despite all the pain, I wouldn't change a thing because even my mistakes taught me valuable life lessons. I now have the experience to trust the next step. You are more powerful than you realize.

How can you recognize your intuition? Think of a time when you knew the answer to something but couldn't prove how you knew what you knew. That's intuition. Your ego mind becomes fearful when you have this type of experience. It wants to make sure that doesn't happen again. I know that when I had clarity about a person or situation I felt complete, whole, and expansive. Even when I felt my life was falling apart, I knew everything would work out more than all right, but I couldn't prove it. I had to act on blind faith. On the surface it felt scary doing something foreign. However I'd remind myself that whatever I'd done until that point in time wasn't working for me. The only way to get a different result was to do things differently.

I learned that when my intuition guided me it was a bad idea for me to share the intuitive guidance I received before taking the action. Have you ever had a great idea, shared it with someone and then felt like the wind had been taken out of your sails? That is what happens when you share intuition instead of taking actions you're meant to take.

I often felt frustrated and abandoned. I wondered why it had to be so difficult. I thought God was making me jump through hoops. None of what I felt, wondered, or thought was true. It was my distorted perception. It was what I chose to see. Whenever I experience a block now, I know that I have to go deeper inside of myself. I have to remove the next layer of what is blocking me from seeing what I need to see in order to get the solutions that will move me forward in my life.

Have you ever felt like someone in your life was stopping you from achieving your goals? Have you ever felt powerless to change a situation in your life because of another person's actions? Do you feel you would be happy if only someone you loved would behave differently? If you answer yes to any of these questions, you have a blind spot—and likely more than one. It's up to you to ask your soul to be shown the deepest parts of yourself. This is how you will receive all the answers you need. The healing will be gentle if you don't wait till you are in so much pain.

This means that when an uncomfortable situation arises you must address it immediately. The longer you put it off, the worse it will get because you are allowing time for the energy to become locked into your body at a cellular level. It then takes longer to remove the block than when you are in the flow of your life.

It takes courage to do this. But you can do it. Feeling temporarily out of sorts is better than having a dull, growing, and consistent pain. When you discover the answer you give yourself power to take action. There is no one else to blame in your life for how things turn out. It's all you, all your responsibility.

This is what people fear the most. That's why they chose to stay blind. Those people think it's the pain-free choice. It's actually compromising the integrity and desire of the soul. This can be experienced as depression and lack of life purpose.

Let your vision guide you. Open yourself to wise intuitive guidance. Your intuition won't let you down.

For years, I strengthened my intuition the hard way. I would receive intuitive guidance and ignore it. Then I would feel awful, because my intuition was correct. A good example is receiving strong intuition that a guy I was attracted to would be bad boyfriend material. My surface desire usually outweighed my intuition. I'd date the guy and end up hurt and confused. That's how I learned to trust my intuition. I'd stick my hand in the flame, burn it, berate myself, and vow never to put myself in pain again. But of course, the flame easily mesmerized me, so once again I'd burn myself. The only way I stopped putting my hand in the fire was when I jumped into the fire of emotional pain and got so badly incinerated that I knew never to ignore my intuition again.

I don't regret my choices. They made me who I am today. I love my life. All these experiences led me to my marriage and the close relationships I have with my family and friends. But there's an easier way. You don't have to put yourself through the shame and low self-esteem I experienced. You can start heeding your intuition right away.

It took me a long time to understand that spirit guides and guardian angels have a different set of priorities than ours. I used to be frustrated when I'd ask my guides about what to do next in a love relationship and they would give me advice about my mindset. At the time, I couldn't understand what detachment had to do with a guy treating me respectfully. Now it is obvious to me: Transform yourself and your life changes.

When you have a blind spot, it can be impossible to embrace the simplest of principles. The way I began to gain immense clarity was by giving psychic readings. It's always easier to see what is best for others, because your emotions are not in the way. In the process of doing readings, I understood more about how spirit guides communicate. When someone who was financially challenged would ask me, "When do you see money coming in?" the person asking expected me to give a specific date. For example, that he would receive $20,000 on June 20, 2010. I learned that spirit doesn't work that way. First spirit tells you the blocks you need to remove to create the space for the $20,000 to be placed into your bank account, and then spirit gives suggestions as to what you need to do next to receive $20,000 because you have free will. I realized that was what was happening in my life, too. They were showing me my blocks and helping me receive.

In the past it upset me when people were terrified because they feared I might tell them something that could ruin their life. My dear friend Andrew Flynn invited me to the premier of the movie *King Arthur* at The Guildhall in London back in 2004. I was excited when I saw Ioan Gruffudd, an actor who stars in *The Fantastic Four* with Jessica Alba. Andrew introduced me and when I told Ioan I hosted a psychic TV show, he said, "You're not really a psychic?" I said, "Yes, I am." He looked like he'd seen someone with the bubonic plague. I tried to ally his fear. "Ioan, a psychic reading is preventive medicine. It helps you see any blocks you may be creating, so you can change the things in your future that aren't working."

"That stuff freaks me out," was his reply. "I don't want to know anything about my future. Nothing," he said firmly, backing away. I felt like a leper. I put on a pretend smile to hide the crap feeling I had inside of me and disappeared into the party crowd.

Another time, a client asked me about her new boyfriend, "Is he 'The One?'" and her spirit guides said, "No." I dreaded her reaction since I knew she was head over heels in love with the guy. I felt like I was a messenger about to be shot. Her spirit guides explained in detail all the reasons why this man was not "The One" and revealed snippets of her future to comfort and inspire her. But all she focused on was the no. To her, it was the end of her world. She couldn't hear spirit's wisdom and she couldn't feel her guides' love and healing support, because she was scared to see the truth. This is what kept her stuck. "Why can't he be 'The One?'" she persisted.

"He can be 'The One,' but he isn't the one for you," I said.

"Can't you tell the guides to make him 'The One'?" she said.

"Spirit would never interfere in the life of another. We all have free will. The only time a relationship or situation in your life can be destiny is when you have made a soul contract before you were born," I answered.

"Tell the guides I want to change my contract. I want him. I can't live without him."

I looked to my client's spirit guides to see if there was any way her soul contract could be changed. I could feel her angst and pain in my own body and I wanted it to stop. I turned back to her. "The only time a soul contract can be changed is when your intention is totally pure, meaning 100 percent love, and you are both willing to experience deeper life lessons and truths from being together. In your situation, your guides are expressing that it is more important for you to first give love to yourself before you can share your life with another. The man you love is not capable of receiving the love you want to give. It would be wasted on him because he is emotionally closed."

"I don't want to end up alone. Why can't the guides get him to feel the love I have for him?" she asked.

"You won't end up alone. Why do want to be with someone who is not capable of loving you the way you want?"

"He does love me. He told me he loves me," she said, desperation in her voice. The truth was sinking in and she didn't want to see it. She'd do anything to stay blind.

"There's a big difference between lust and love. Bonding hormones stay in your body for three weeks after you've made love. If he really loves you, why isn't he calling you and why is he dating someone else? Are you sure you love him?" I said. I felt like I was talking to myself. I'd been in my client's situation and I remembered feeling exactly how she felt, except this time I understood that the spirit guides were giving guidance.

I used to think my guides were punishing me, making me suffer because I'd done something wrong, and that because of this I didn't deserve love. I now know without a doubt that wasn't true. Helping my clients led me to see this truth.

I could see clear as day that my client had so much love to give. She was wide open and vulnerable. This man she'd hoped was "The One" for her had opened her heart. He was the preparation for her meeting "The One." When she left, I wrote out a prayer and placed it under a pink rose quart crystal that my friend Pam gave to me as a gift, and I lit a candle for my client. As I prayed for this woman, I gave thanks to my spirit guides and God that they had my best interests at heart. It was then that I knew to trust the guidance I received, even if it wasn't the guidance I wanted. I knew all would turn out well if my client and me followed spirit's lead.

A year later, I bumped into that client in Santa Monica. She looked like a different person. "You were right about my boyfriend. It took me about six months to finally let go of him, but when I did I met someone three months later. Our relationship is amazing. I never believed I could meet someone so loving and kind. I now see why I settled before. My new boyfriend is taking me away to the desert this weekend. I'm so happy. Thank you," she said.

I was elated to see her happy and truly in love. This is why I do what I do. This is what inspires me to teach people how to receive their own guidance. My client had done all the work on herself following her psychic reading. All I had done was to show her how and she mustered the courage to take a look at her blind spots and remove them.

Another area of life in which people get incredibly stuck is their career. One of my clients is at the top of his field. There's no higher level to be promoted to, and he hates his job. He seemingly has everything and yet he's empty inside. Another client is working in an office doing administrative work to pay the bills. She has no motivation to seek any other opportunities because she feels she's not worthy, talented, or skilled enough to do anything else.

When you compromise the creativity of your heart, your soul stagnates. When I investigated deeper using my clairvoyance to look at both of these clients' blind spots, what came to light is that this man had given up on his dream of building furniture and being an artist. "I can't make a living painting. I wouldn't know where to start, besides I have a family to support and bills to pay."

My female client said, "I don't have any life purpose because I don't know what else I can achieve."

"I know you have a life purpose. You're blocking yourself from seeing it. If you could do anything what would you do?" I said.

She had to think about this before answering and when she did, I saw sparks of white light appear in her aura. "I've always wanted to travel to exotic places."

"Anything else?" I said.

"I was taking guitar and singing lessons. Except I gave up last year," she said.

"Why?" I said.

"My allergies were affecting my voice. I decided there was no point continuing," she said.

"If you could play the guitar and sing, what would you do with your talent?" I said.

"Blind Vision": You Have All the Answers, So Why Can't You See Your Blocks and Limitations?

"I'd play rock to an audience at The Universal Amphitheatre and sell my CDs," she said.

"So you do have a life purpose," I said.

"No, it's silly. I don't see how I can do it," she said.

"You can do it. If that's what you want?" I said.

"That would be great," she said.

"All you have to do now is put a plan together and take the steps to make it happen. I know you can do it."

As an intuition coach and psychic medium, I can see a person's true essence. Someone may be a banker or a housewife and I can look at his or her energy and know that his or her life purpose is to be a senator or a motivational speaker. A production assistant I worked with at MTV popped into my head the other day. She's excellent at creating systems. My intuition told me she'd be running a big company one day. All she has to do is embrace the value of who she is and then it'll happen fast. It's a painful and liberating feeling when it dawns upon you that the only person stopping you from achieving your dreams is you.

It's painful because you could feel remorse for not having taken action sooner. From another perspective, it's liberating. It means you can make everything you want happen now.

We all create barriers and blocks. These are what stop us from seeing the answers we need. You can live your life purpose now. The first step is saying yes to that purpose, and then removing one block at a time mindfully until all blocks are released.

Your circumstances and mindset determine the length of time it will take to release a block. There are many factors involved. This is why when a client asks, "When will I meet my future husband?" or "Will I get an acting role soon?" it is difficult to put a specific date on the manifestation unless it is pre-destined. Ninety-five percent of your life is free will. Energy is constantly changing and you cannot control other people's actions. We created the Gregorian calendar to pinpoint time, however energy is not ruled by this date and time system. Energy is constantly active and transforming.

The way to create more accurate timing in your life is to plan and take very specific and targeted steps. If you miss one of your targets, you have to reassess the energy patterns and cycles you're in, and quickly take a new action step.

One of my client's couldn't get herself out of debt. Every time she'd make some money, an unexpected bill would arise and she was back to square one. "How come other people are okay financially and I can't even make $500 a week, let alone shoot for my first million?" she questioned.

I closed my eyes and focused in on her energy. Most of her aura and energy body were gold, the color of abundance and wisdom, however when I began to peel back the layers of her energy, looking deeper and deeper, I could see chunks of black and grey energy in her aura that were representing negative thought forms and stagnation.

During hypnosis, a hypnotist guides the person deeper and deeper inside. The hypnotist knows whatever is holding the patient back is at a deep unconscious level or else the patient would not be experiencing a fear or block in his or her life. The only difference in what I do is that I can psychically see the energy block. I look at this energy and determine the specific meaning of the block. Usually it is a negative thought form created by the client. We then remove the block together by pinpointing the uncomfortable energy in the physical body and reflecting upon the thought form associated with it. Awareness of the energy is a catalyst for releasing the cycle of pain. It unravels and then we visualize golden light replacing the space where the pain was, and seed a new concept to support the manifestation of life purpose.

There are many different clearing techniques you could use. Which is the best depends on the circumstances of the moment. In chapter 8, I'll go into greater detail.

You can do this for yourself, too. Anyone can do this. The most important thing to be aware of is that as soon as you remove a block, a vacuum of space is created that can feel uncomfortable. Our reflex is to fill that space back up. If you do not have a purpose or intention, the old block returns. This is why many people are enthusiastic about losing excess pounds and getting fit, yet end up putting all the weight they've lost back on and making unsatisfactory improvements.

Once a block is removed, it is crucial to develop blind faith so that you can create a new result for yourself. This could take a week or it could take a year depending on your thoughts, feelings, and environment. It took me a year to reach my goal of fitting into a size 6 dress. There were many times I'd get on the scale or look at myself in the mirror, pinch a piece of fat, and think to myself, "It's not working." Thankfully, my intuition spoke to me softly and firmly, "You're on track. You will get the results you want because you are exercising five days a week and you are eating sensibly."

The key is to create a specific goal before you remove a block. This will give you the motivation to follow through once you've removed the block. Your biggest challenge will be to stop the block from returning, not removing it. This is why a healer cannot heal you. Only you can heal yourself. The healer's role is to support you, be a witness, and hold you accountable to the transformation you are creating within yourself.

It took me thirty-two years to remove my blocks about being able to give and receive love, and another year to discover what love meant to me before I was able to experience the love I had only ever thought existed in fairytales.

Use the same principle to create success. No one stops you from getting a small business loan, signing a big client, or booking the movie role of your dreams. It's all you. The sooner you trust that you have every resource you need inside of you to have everything you want, it will happen. Your intuition will guide you to know best how and where to invest your time. As mega-successful entrepreneur Alex Mandossian says, "Outsource and delegate what you don't love." When you follow this advice, you'll one day notice that any blocks you once had have finally disappeared.

The Three Biggest Problems in Trusting Your Intuition

When you begin to experience the power of yourself, it is truly uplifting. You can feel like you are on Cloud 9. Things that bothered you before become unimportant. This frees up energy for you to focus on creating the life you want. However three big problems can block you from trusting your intuition. You can keep these at bay only if you don't shirk from them and instead tackle them head on. Sticking your head in the sand is not a solution.

The first problem in trusting your intuition is the responsibility you undertake once you trust your intuition, especially when other people are affected by your choices.

- What if you buy the wrong home and can't sell it later on?

- What if he seems perfect, you have a child together, and then he turns out to be a womanizer?

- What if you leave the law firm right before they offer you partnership?

- What if you assumed your best friend was trying to steal your boyfriend when her intentions were to protect you and you lost two people you love?

These are the sorts of challenges that can arise, and this is when you need to use and trust your intuition to ensure you do what's best for yourself and everyone involved. Of course you have to be responsible with your intuition. You must never manipulate or try to control someone with your intuitive guidance. It is not about getting one up over someone who you perceive as arrogant. It is not your responsibility to teach someone a lesson because they treat others badly. Your responsibility is to be totally focused on your thoughts, feelings, motivations, and actions.

When you take this approach and you ask yourself:

- Are my intentions pure?

- Do I want what is best for everyone involved in this situation?

- Is the intuitive guidance I'm receiving in alignment with my heart's desire?

If the answer to any of these questions is no, the responsibility you have will feel like a ton of lead. You will become fearful about making a choice when there is a block within you. The way to remove the block is to get quiet, close your eyes, go deeper within yourself and ask each one of the questions above again. This will reveal to you why you are fearful of the responsibility of your intuition.

A powerful affirmation to remove this obstacle is: "It is safe for me to be responsible. I have everyone's best interests at heart. I always take the best action."

Whenever you need to make an important decision and you want to call upon your intuition say the affirmation above to create the energetic shift you need to open yourself up to guidance.

The second big problem in trusting your intuition is your interpretation of the information you receive. Remember how I shared with you earlier on about the psychic medium that asked me if I knew someone with a red sports car and came up with a stupid answer? To become truly skilled at trusting your intuition, you will need to develop your own language of communication with your guardian angels and spirit guides.

The way spirit perceives information and how they feel it is different from us. There is always a period of miscommunication as you learn this new skill. It takes time to develop and the way you develop it is by practicing. I know that when I first learned to speak French all I understood was "Hello, how are you?" and "Goodbye." Soon I could manage basic conversations. But if someone launched into a story, I could barely keep up. I only caught every other word, like table, sun, sleep, or different, but I didn't know how to put the information together. I was frustrated.

Sometimes the person talking to me would use big dramatic hand movements to help me, much like spirit gives clairvoyant images as a comparison. I'd repeat back how I understood what they said, hoping I didn't sound like a complete idiot. But if I hadn't grasped it, they would have to explain it from a different angle until I did get it. Similarly, spirit guides use metaphors to help us understand energy. This enables us to make abstract, intangible energy, coherent and tangible.

I'm always delighted when I see someone in my intuition development class take a risk to decipher information and share their interpretation of it with someone else. It takes courage to do this. No one likes to feel stupid, however it's common to feel this way at first when you begin to use your intuitive muscle. A good affirmation to remove this fear is: "I am attuned to higher communication. I see all I need to see. I know the best action to take. I trust my intuition and I communicate it clearly."

The third big problem with trusting your intuition is looking outside of yourself for the answers. This is the fastest way to make you uncertain and insecure. Only you know the full circumstances of your situation. All you have to do is look at every aspect of your situation from as many angles as possible until you experience clarity from within yourself.

Have you ever felt confident about a decision you are about to follow through on and rather than trust your inner guidance asked someone else if they think you're taking the right action? One of my clients got herself in a right old pickle doing that. She was confused about her job status. She wanted to leave, but a year later still hadn't followed her gut instinct even though her work environment was taking an increasing toll on her health. "I know I should leave the job but I can't," she said.

"What's stopping you?" I said.

"I don't know. I'm confused," she said.

Where confusion is at play, so are other people's perceptions. It turned out she'd made a decision to leave her job and felt good about it until she shared the news with her parents who asked, "Are you sure that's a wise move? What if you can't get another job? You're in a competitive market. Someone else would love to be in your position."

My client defended her position. She told me she had still been upbeat and went on to share the news with her new boyfriend. They'd been dating for three months and everything was going great. She was sure he'd be supportive. Instead he responded, "Why leave your job when you're so good at what you do? It's paying you a top salary and it won't be easy to get back in the loop if you decide to go back."

This was not what my client had anticipated. She thought he was spontaneous and romantic. Fear set in as she heard his words echo, "It won't be easy to get back in the loop if you decide to go back."

That weekend, she hung out with a good girlfriend. They went for a coffee and she hoped that she would get reassurance that her intuition was absolutely correct that it was the right thing to leave her job. She vented about her parents' and boyfriends comments about her decision. Her friend said, "If the people who care for you most are concerned about your choice, maybe they've got a point. You've got a great job. Hell, I'd do anything to be an executive in a movie studio and you've got a new man. Why rock the boat?"

"Maybe you're right," my client said.

As we sat together, before I'd even begun the psychic reading, I'd received a very strong impression that her job wasn't in alignment with her heart's desire, although it seemed great on the surface. It would be best to leave. However it would take courage for her to step outside of her comfort zone. When I told her so, my client sighed with relief. "So I wasn't imagining everything. My intuition was correct?"

"Yes," I said.

My client went on to hand in her notice to the studio and produce her own independent film and she was so much happier. All the advice she'd received only got her stuck. She'd needed to trust her intuition.

When you begin using your intuition, the worst thing you can do is ask someone else if it's right. What is right for one person isn't for everyone else. Your situation is always unique, as are you. It is important to note that your intuition may guide you to do more research before making a decision. Only ask a mentor who has been in a similar situation before for guidance, and only take what is applicable to your situation into consideration.

Think back to past decisions you've needed to make. Review who the people were that you asked for advice. This will give you very telling information that will help you build confidence in your own intuition.

An appropriate affirmation to overcome the problem of looking outside of yourself for the answers is: "I have access to all the answers I need. It is safe for me to be self-reliant. I know what to do next."

Three Simple Techniques to See the Truth of a Situation

There are numerous techniques you can apply to help you gain clarity. At times, life can get very busy and stressful and it's hard to see what your next best move is. Here are three simple steps to guide you towards the answers you need:

Step #1: Take a couple of deep breaths, close your eyes, and ask yourself, "How does my body feel regarding this situation?" Here's a specific example, "What sensations am I experiencing in my body when I think about leaving my job?"

It is best to write down the insights that come from this inquiry because this helps bring unconscious energy into your awareness. For example, "I have a dropping feeling in my stomach, my mouth feels dry, and I feel overwhelmed."

Each sensation has a different meaning, depending on where the feeling is in your body. I discuss this in greater detail from two different perspectives in chapters 5 and 8.

Step #2: Ask: "What is my next best step?" As you ask and answer this question, pretend that you are giving advice to a stranger. This will help you to perceive your situation from a position of detachment. The more emotional you feel about a person or situation, the harder it will be to receive clear intuitive guidance. You are looking for a new action to take that is intuitively guided.

Here's an example of how this has worked well for me. A while ago, I called my dad for support. My ex-fiancé had approached me on my in-person client day at the Aura Shop, even though I'd written to him asking him to leave me alone.

"You're unsettled," Dad said.

"I'm okay," I said, "but frustrated that he won't let me get on with my life."

"That's unsettled," Dad said.

"How do I let this go once and for all?" I said.

"Be your own coach, that's what you do for other people, right?"

"Yes, it's easy for me to get guidance for other people," I said.

"Well, you can do it for yourself. Pretend you are a client coming to see you for a solution and then follow that guidance," Dad said pragmatically.

"I can do that," I said, as my stomach turned. His comment triggered me because the solution was simple. When I'd previously asked my ex-fiancé to leave me alone a small part of my unconscious remained attached to being paid back the money I had lent him. Even though I had consciously written off the debt 100 percent, that part of me was still hopeful. When I looked at the situation from the perspective of reading for a client it led me to the question, "Why would a man who owes you $400,000 pay you the money now when he's been making that same empty promise for ten years?"

The answer came through loud and clear as a bell with no emotion, "He wouldn't." That presented me with an action step I hadn't taken before: Delete all his emails and block his email address. If I ever bumped into him in the street, I decided I would not converse with him. If he tried to engage in conversation, I would call 9-1-1. I felt a little awkward because this was an action I had never considered. It was outside of my comfort zone. The newness confirmed to me that the guidance was good.

Step #3: Ask: "Why is this a good action to take?"

I spoke with Dad a few days later and told him about my discovery. I wanted to have someone I trusted to hold me accountable by being a witness to my decision. I knew this new behavior could be challenging for me even though I am happily married now, because I had weakened my position so many times in the past regarding this man. That's how I had poured $400,000 down the drain in the first place.

"Are you sure?" Dad said.

"Absolutely, I know this is the best action for me. It means I can once and for all forgive myself for the past mistakes I made. It allows me to close that chapter on my life. I know that I am not my past mistakes. I was doing my best at the time and things went badly because I was fearful. The blessing here is that if things had been different, I would have married him. I wouldn't have met Nick and I wouldn't have Winston, Stella, and Courvoisier as my animal companions."

"That's good. I can hear it in your voice. You sound at peace," Dad said.

"Finally, I am," I said.

Completion Step #4: Sleep on it. In the morning, or in a week, if it still seems like the clear, strong, and peaceful right next step to you, act upon it.

When I did this last step regarding my ex-fiancé I wanted to ensure I was making the right choice. Making a break in communication is final. Being prepared to take a tough action if I ever bumped into this man was a strong action commitment to make. Because it felt solid and clear I knew it was the right action. I gave myself a week to sit with the energy and to let it settle. Then I followed through on my action and it felt great. As I blocked the emails I felt the parts of my life that ex-fiancé had criticized return to me. The good memories of my past rushed back to me in a heartbeat. I was proud of who I was. I had unearthed a new confidence from within and I know that is a gift for keeps.

When I come up against an internal block I don't often go to others for advice. I share my vulnerability with those close to me, especially my husband Nick. But he doesn't tell me what to do. He's an excellent listener and supporter. As I get my thoughts and fears out of my head and have him or a dear friend witness my internal process, I feel like a weight is being lifted from me. Then my answers come from within.

I've learned not to confide in people who like giving advice. They mean well but they don't know what's best for my situation. I recommend you share your heart with people who will happily listen to you. That doesn't mean complain to them about your situation. Instead, get your feelings out of your system once, so you can see how things look from an outside perspective. People who want to get busy in your life usually have a lot of pain and problems in their own lives and they believe they will feel better about themselves if they can focus on your challenges. This doesn't help you or them. Distance yourself from these types of destructive communication patterns or you could end up in a series of unhealthy, codependent relationships.

The best time to seek outside guidance rather than trusting your own intuition is when you feel overwhelmed or at an impasse. Guidance in the form of loving support will calm your soul and align you with your intuition. At times we all need support. We're human beings, not super heroes. In the past, I thought because of my role as a psychic medium I had to be perfect. I was terrified of what people would think of me if they knew I was having challenges in my own life. I thought they wouldn't be able to trust me to support them because of my weaknesses. Many of my friends came to me for psychic readings and I unknowingly isolated myself more and more from them. This was a painful realization. I became ultra-sensitive in social settings. Yes me, the London party girl. I seemed accepting of people's problems on the surface, but my unconscious was judgmental because all of the pain building up inside me.

In the next chapter I will talk about healing pain in detail because I want to ensure that as you develop your intuition and become more sensitive you keep yourself open. That doesn't mean when you meet a complete stranger tell them your life's history of bad relationships or your beliefs about religion. Go slowly, gently, and honestly in forming connections and you will build solid trustworthy relationships.

Some of my clients have expressed how they have no friends they feel safe to turn to, and that they feel alone and misunderstood. I've told those people that they're not the only ones who feel that way. Reach out and connect to people. Practice being a good listener. Even if your mind wanders when you're listening, holding space for someone else will make you feel good.

If you ever hit a low and feel awfully depressed, drag yourself out to an event. It will stop you from focusing on the size of your problems if you are engaging with other people. Al-Anon meetings are a great place to go. Whenever my energy has felt depleted, that is where I go to fill back up with love and to reconnect to my life purpose.

The Two Most Important Things You Must Do Now to Stop Future Problems

The two most important things you must do today to ensure you don't encounter problems in the future are to address your denial and to take a new course of action.

First, address your denial. Denial stops you from seeing what you need to see. It keeps you from knowing what you need to do. When I first began writing this book, I was worried about what I would share. Whenever a client asked me a question or I gave information in a workshop I could easily share my insights, however as soon as I'd sit down at my laptop to write I would hit a wall.

It was absolutely clear to me that I had a blind spot that was very painful for me to look at. I was keeping myself busy with clients and workshops, and denying the problem while inside my soul was screaming, "The book Joanna. You've got to write the book!"

I completed a book cover because I thought that would motivate me to write, but it didn't. I thought if I pre-sold the book and orders came in, I'd be able to write. That didn't motivate me either. The reason it didn't work was that I was trying to be someone I was not. I phoned my dear friend Kim Castle and said, "Kim, I'm blocking myself. I have a responsibility to finish this book. I love writing. But every time I sit down to write, I go blank. I know I'm in denial."

"What's the purpose of your book?" Kim asked me.

"I want to empower people to trust their own intuition," I told her.

"What's stopping you?" she asked.

Having Kim as a witness helped me face my denial. "I'm scared what people will think," I said. "That's what holds me back."

"If you give yourself permission to be vulnerable, perhaps you'll be able to write the book," Kim suggested.

My stomach flipped, so I knew she was right. I had to give myself permission to write this book and to be vulnerable in the process. That is how I finally wrote this book and that's why I've dedicated a whole chapter to permission. If I hadn't had that heart to heart chat with Kim, this book would not be in your hands right now.

The second thing to do to prevent future problems from arising is to set out upon a new course of action. This is important because the way you've been doing things until now hasn't been working well for you if you have a problem. You have to take a new approach to get what you want.

In my own life, to ensure I would complete this book I had to embrace a new attitude. In the past, I thought that putting myself first was selfish and that I needed to be on-call for my clients whenever they needed a psychic phone reading. The repercussions of this mindset were that I never had enough creative space in my mind to write and bring all the knowledge from my head onto the page. I thought I was being of service to others when I compromised my creativity. The new course of action I committed to was to only check my email and voicemail once a day. When I told some people that I was doing this they looked at me with concern—especially those who are attached to their Blackberry's. But they very quickly learned that it was okay. Having time to write was fantastic.

Writing this book showed me how to see the bigger picture. It gave me perspective on my life. I realized that part of my fear was that if I weren't available 24/7, people wouldn't want to connect with me anymore. It felt odd to turn away clients. I thought that they'd feel I didn't care. Quite the contrary. I wanted the opportunity to share as much information about intuition as possible with as many people as possible.

Every time I hit a bump in my road as I embraced my new approach, such as feeling fearful because my income was lowering, I would remind myself, "Joanna, this bump is because of an old past action you took. It won't happen again because you are doing things differently now. Keep moving forwards with the new action. It is the right action to take. You will see." Sure enough, my blind faith has paid off dividends.

Is there a project or goal that you still haven't completed because you feel you haven't got the time or resources to get it done? If I, who was the Queen procrastinator can get things done, you most definitely can too. I invite you to pick one goal around something you'd truly love to achieve. Go through the four-step process I just taught and identify all the things holding you back. Come up with an action step to take on behalf of each item on your list. Follow your plan and you will soon achieve your goal.

Chapter 5

HEALING PAIN

"Healing takes courage, and we all have courage, even if we have to dig a little to find it." —Tori Amos

As a psychic medium, I see pain as multidimensional energy. People don't have to tell me they are in pain for me to feel their pain. When I'm in the presence of a person who carries a lot of pain I feel like a large ball of lead has been placed on my back. Other times I sense the life force barely present in people. I know they are doing their best just to survive the pain. I have to admit that when I got to this chapter, I wanted to skip over it. Pain is not something we ever want to feel, however it is an indicator that shows you when you are off track in your life or you are making poor decisions.

The Purpose of Pain's Guidance

Have you ever had the experience when someone inside your physical boundaries made you feel sick? Last night at the gym, another member began chatting with me. On the surface this person was bright and gregarious, however when he shook my hand to say goodnight severe nausea ran through my body. From an intuitive perspective, pain is energy that is out of harmony with your heart, spirit, and soul. When you ignore pain its energy condenses, intensifies, and amplifies.

Pain can be experienced on any one of the physical, emotional, mental, or spiritual planes or it can be experienced on all levels simultaneously. It depends on the situation. The first step to remove pain is to recognize what type of pain you are experiencing and on how many of the energetic planes.

When I feel pain, I know it is telling me to sit up and pay attention. I've learned that when I embrace it, I shift into a state of inner peace. Being aware of the energy field around you and how you are responding to it is the key to leading a pain-free life.

If you feel pain around a person or a situation, it is not your responsibility to take on that person's pain or to solve the situation. That is not the purpose of pain. But often it is what healers and empathetic people do naturally. I had to train myself not to absorb other people's energy. With practice you'll learn how to do the same. Your challenge is to stay open and maintain your energy boundaries at the same time. It is possible.

The energy of pain is dense, however it can move quickly when it senses it isn't welcome in your being anymore. Then it will move to another part of your body or soul. If you've ever received a healing modality called Reiki and you are sensitive and aware of energy, you may sense that as the pain lifts from one part of your body it is then felt in another part of your body. This is because pain can exist many layers deep. When I have received bodywork, Reiki, or shamanic energy work, I can see, hear, and feel the pain. I can see the pain energy release from my body. As it leaves I receive an impression of why the pain was in my body and what it means.

Sometimes you will need to review your pain and understand it intellectually for it to release from your body. Other times you can let it go without needing to look into the past. The lesson you needed to learn has already been learned and the pain is merely the residue of a past experience that is not relevant to you now. It is still there only because it has been trapped in your body. When you begin to understand different types of pain that exist and you develop a deeper understanding of the quality and resonance of your pain, you will be able to break down the pain and remove it effectively.

Do you get tired often? Or do you experience headaches? These are the two most common types of pain. When you get tired, your body or soul is letting you know that you are positioning yourself to take on pain. Getting tired is a warning sign that you are about to move out of balance. There are several different types of tiredness: exhaustion, lethargy, irritation, nervousness, distraction, paralysis, and vacancy.

Remember pain is only energy in different parts of your being. Everyone carries pain. Your challenge is when pain is not apparent to you. Meanwhile it lies very deep within your being and influences your actions. I remember being dreamy and high when I was dating one guy, however, when it didn't work out, I felt like a black hole had been opened up in my stomach and that a veil of lead had been thrown over me. I thought I'd taken on the guy's energy (this can be the case), however as I more closely investigated the origination of the energy, I discovered this energy was already present within me at a deep unconscious level. My feelings for the guy had increased my sensitivity to pain because the energy of love had opened me to experiencing more aliveness and presence.

A headache can be telling about your mindset and the unconscious limiting thoughts you have on a daily basis. Taking analgesics to relieve pain desensitizes you from being able to release those thoughts. When you get a headache, it's your mind and body telling you, "What you are doing or thinking is taking you out of alignment with your heart."

When pain kicks in, you need to enter into introspection. This is the first step if you want to release a pain blockage. I say, "want," because at an unconscious level, many people thrive on pain and don't want to let it go. Their pain has become habitual. They fear that there is no alternative to support them in feeling good. There is always an option. If you cannot find it, you can create it. Of course, this is often easier said than done. However, with a commitment to your well-being, and through serious introspection about the reasons for pain, you will get positive results.

Recognizing Pain

You can recognize illness and stop it from developing within you if you become adept at spotting the first signs of pain. Most people think of pain as something sharp, intense, and agonizing. Pain can be subtle, so subtle that you barely notice it. When it's there, its stops you from having the kind of constant, clear flow of energy that creates balanced emotions and perfect health. Oftentimes pain begins as tiredness. That's why a good night's sleep or an afternoon meditation is regenerative. Pain also begins if you take on someone's negative feeling about you, or if you feel negatively about someone.

Think of a time when someone made a comment that hurt your feelings. Can you remember how you felt? When my feelings are hurt, my stomach drops for a moment, and I sense my aura going gray and shrinking towards my body. I know that if I don't do something quickly, the painful experience will stick like cement in my body. When this happens I carve out the time to exercise at the gym, go for a walk, or do a meditation. As I'm working out or meditating, I sense the bad feeling breaking into tiny pieces and then falling away.

Sound toning is another great way to release pain. Just hum or sing one long note of "ah." The vibration of your voice will dislodge blocks that exist deep inside of you. Listening to your favorite music also will lift and expand your energy field, allowing you to breakthrough any negative thoughts and blocks that are causing you pain.

One of the benefits of meditation is that you can use it to develop the sensitivity to recognize pain before it has the chance to get comfortable in your body and energy field.

It's never an accident when you have an accident. A series of thoughts and experiences form a specific vibration in you, which creates an accident. When I was eleven years old, I tripped outside my classroom, fell hard, and fractured my left wrist. On the surface I was just a kid running with books in my hand when I should have been walking. At an unconscious level, I was worried because I realized that my parents were heading towards a separation. My fractured wrist ended up being the catalyst for their divorce.

For about four years after that I remember thinking that if I didn't have my accident, they wouldn't have divorced. I thought it was my fault that their marriage ended because my dad had already planned to go on a skiing trip and Mom gave him an ultimatum, "If you go while Joanna's wrist is fractured, I want a divorce." Dad asked me if I was okay with him going on the skiing vacation. I said, "Yes." My parents divorced.

Whether or not I had fractured my wrist, my parents' relationship was already fractured. My accident was merely a catalyst for bringing the emotional pain we were all feeling to the surface faster than before. They would have divorced in any case. I had the accident because I didn't know another way to release the pain that was building up inside me. I ignored the internal pain until it got my attention.

If you have pain at any level, whether it is emotional or physical, listen to it. It's trying to tell you to get in alignment with your higher self or to live your life purpose.

People often struggle to get rid of pain without finding the cause of it. Some rush straight to the doctor, others take homeopathic remedies. My clients often ask me to read their energy (or the energy of loved ones) and diagnose their pain, and ask for suggestions on how best to remove it. At an energetic level, I can see the developmental stages of pain. This helps me determine if a client needs a medicine, a homeopathic remedy, a healing treatment (for example, Reiki, shiatsu, or deep tissue massage), or to do exercise, like yoga and Pilates, to bring internal harmony to mind, body, and spirit.

Medical Conditions

If you have suffered clinical depression, schizophrenia or have a chemical imbalance in your brain and are taking any medications, it is best to move forward very gently with the development of your sixth sense. Diving in too fast could trigger trauma and stress. It is best to find a local meditation or yoga class to attend while you are beginning to practice these skills so you are in a supportive environment.

Let me be very clear that I'm not a medical professional. I am able to read energy, but the information I offer is only an adjunct to professional medical guidance. An intuitive medical reading is like icing on a cake when someone has tried everything they can think of and they're stuck. If you are experiencing a health related or psychological condition, please consult your health care professional. It can be dangerous to ignore a medical condition or to stop taking medication without guidance.

When my intuition intensified at twenty-one years of age, I repeatedly got migraine headaches across the front of my forehead and felt waves of nausea whenever I was in a crowd of people, especially when I had to take the subway to work. Sometimes I needed to sleep for fourteen hours at a stretch. For short periods, I would become extremely sensitive to sound and I'd flinch if someone went to touch me. On those occasions I felt like a Woody Allen character. I turned into an absolute hypochondriac. Thankfully I lived within a five-minute walk of my doctor's office so I could schedule frequent appointments for myself. I'd give the doctor my list of symptoms. Then he would carry out an examination and tell me, "There's nothing wrong with you."

"But I feel sick and I have all these symptoms," I said.

"Okay, I'll run tests," he said.

All the tests came back negative, but my pain symptoms persisted. I went to three other doctors over a period of four years and each doctor told me I was in perfect health. You'd think I'd be grateful, but I wasn't. I was frustrated that I so often felt awful and had no proof of a condition to back up my symptoms. I didn't yet understand that I was experiencing pain and illness before it had manifested into physical form. That

117

was why the doctors couldn't detect anything. What I needed to do was to look at what was causing the pain inside me and resolve it energetically.

Depending on the circumstances, conventional medicine is helpful. I have the utmost respect for doctors, nurses, and surgeons. There are times when medication is necessary, such as when a patient cannot overcome a physical illness without, for example, the support of antibiotics. I recommend that in addition to any conventional therapies you are using, you also look at your thoughts and feelings with intuition. It is always up to patients to heal at an emotional level and to transform their mindsets.

I am not a fan of sleeping pills to relieve stress because they shut off the intuition and create an environment for emotional pain to grow. If people have become accustomed to taking sleeping pills and abruptly stop, they not only can experience physical withdraw symptoms, they have heightened emotions to clear. Sudden exposure to buried pain can lead to poor decision-making.

How to Stop Pain from Coming Back

Have you ever had a headache, taken a pain reliever, and had the pain temporarily disappear only to return?

Have you ever felt positive and upbeat one day, and down in the dumps the next?

Have you ever been optimistic about life and sensed you could do anything, followed by a feeling that it's too late for you and nothing is ever going to happen?

Have you had an amazing connection with a guy, and felt as if you were in heaven? He treated you like gold, you were the apple of his eye, and then he ignored you, behaved disrespectfully, didn't include you in his plans, and your emails were moved to his junk mail folder?

We're all constantly experiencing some form of pain, but we often do not realize it because we discount our feelings. Some painful energy is subtle. In general, however, pain becomes more pronounced when you bring light into your body. Your energy cells are constantly vibrating. Let's say you have a good connection with a guy, both your energies extend out to each other and merge, and it feels great. If he then backs off while your energy is several feet outside of you, you'll feel unsupported. He's absorbed and taken part of your good energy (which you gave to him and allowed him to take), and now you're left with pronounced pain in your body. This is a typical scenario, which explains why we can be most unsettled when it comes to matters of the heart.

Everything is energy. What a lover says to you is energy. What you feel is energy. When you start a relationship with someone, you set up patterns of energy within you that are reflected back to you perfectly, so that you and your partner are in symmetry. If you think a romantic partner's energy is off and yet you have attracted this person to you, it's a sign that your energy is also off. Otherwise you wouldn't be having the experience. You both have the same type of pain buried within you on an unconscious level. On the surface everything could look good, and for a time you will resonate and in be harmony. Then the pain that was always present beneath the surface will come into your awareness.

The way to stop pain from returning is to accept its presence. If you have a large piece of pain, for example the pain of sexual or emotional abuse, buried deep in you, you'll find that the soul typically clears it in stages, rather than all at once, as that would be traumatic. Fundamentally we are creatures of habit. We exist in a universe of patterns. Conscious change is more unsettling than life unconsciously happening to you, because suddenly you are acutely aware that you are in control of your destiny.

People most often associate pain with the physical body. For me, the greatest pain I have experienced is emotional. It's up to you to tap into your intuition and receive inner guidance and then take the action steps you are given to release the pain. This ensures that the pain goes away once and for all. How will you respond to pain in your life?

Removing Pain

There are a series of steps you can take to remove pain. The time it takes to release the pain depends on how effectively you are able to immerse yourself in the layers of energy within you. The probability of experiencing a quantum healing, meaning immediate disappearance of an illness (doctors call this *spontaneous remission*), is determined by your ability to handle large amounts of unconscious energy coming into awareness. Ultimately this is why only you can heal yourself. A doctor, a therapist, or an energy healer's role in healing is to help you prepare an energetic environment so that you can release the pain.

Why do you think cancer returns once it has been cut out? Why does someone who has his or her debt paid off by a relative fall back into financial trouble? Why do years of relationship counseling result in a loveless marriage? No one else can get rid of your pain except you.

This realization can be terrifying and overwhelming for some people. It can stop them in their tracks. The great news is that you have an immense resource available within you. You can achieve your heart's desire. No dream is too big when you're willing to be in energetic alignment with spirit. The way I see it from an intuitive perspective is that your pain gives you the opportunity to find wisdom within. You have this ability, too. The greater your loss, the bigger your potential gain. The harder you fall in business, the more opportunity to create a quantum leap in your career. Think of the millionaires you've read about or know. Many have gone bankrupt before hitting their jackpot. People who experience dysfunctional relationships often end up finding true, long-lasting love afterwards. Pain holds important lessons.

When I look back on my most painful experiences, I cherish them. They keep me in gratitude and remind me to maintain higher consciousness. The best thing about pain is that it is a tool for developing greater awareness and aliveness. Until you've lost a fortune it's hard to grasp what being broke really means. I remember a friend telling me she was broke and that life was hard. At that time this woman owned two million dollars worth of real estate and would spend a thousand dollars on a dress without batting an eyelid. Her definition of "broke" and mine were different. What is your perception of broke?

I can only imagine the pain of losing a parent, child, or spouse. I've never felt the pain of loss at a physical level except through feeling these emotions in others during clairsentient readings. One aspect of clairsentience is the ability to feel another person's physical sensations. (In chapter 8, we'll discuss how to stop absorbing other people's pain and negativity.) Many clients who feel compelled to work with me are natural empaths themselves. At times they feel like they are being bombarded by other people's energy. They struggle to connect to their internal source of well-being, as they are running a large amount of pain through them and need help releasing it.

Can you perceive pain beyond a cut, bruise, or headache? Could you become aware of how to let go of pain when you are overwhelmed by it? The key to releasing discomfort is by developing an awareness of its presence in each one of your subtle bodies. You need to focus on the physical body, the emotional body, the mental plane, and the spiritual plane to understand how much pain resides within you. From a psychic perspective, each layer of your being travels for infinity. Each layer is light and pure intelligence. Being psychic alone does not remove pain.

Your mind plays a key role in transforming pain into peace. On a physical level, we perceive consciousness inside the mind. From the standpoint of the sixth sense, your mind has no limits. Your thoughts travel far and wide through time and space in all directions.

At a party someone once asked me, "How can you read someone psychically in Australia who wants to know about the health of a relative in the UK?" My answer was this. I have developed a relationship with my mind that allows me to connect to people beyond how we are used to connecting in everyday life. This didn't happen overnight. It took many years of meditation to open to the expansiveness of my mind, and it was while doing psychic readings that I learned to zone in on specific people's energy.

As you develop this skill, remember that it should only be used for the highest good of all concerned. If you use this ability with the intention of exerting power over someone else, for example, to get revenge, or if you use it to try and make someone love you, it won't work. You will create a black hole of energy in the pit of your stomach that will eat away inside of you. The person you will hurt the most is you. As you develop sensory awareness, a greater sense of responsibility will be instilled in you. Decisions you'd have happily made before will press against the consciousness of your mind.

Meditation breaks down the barrier of the confines of the mind so that spirit and mind become one. If you choose to integrate awareness of the sixth sense into your life, you will increase the flow of love and peace you experience, and these will replace any pain you feel. Releasing pain is a lifelong necessity. You don't clear pain and, that's it, you're finished. You exist in a dimension that has an energetic counterpart that requires constant attention. Fortunately, you can learn to clear energy blocks faster.

The way to remove the pain is to transform it. The way you transform it is by altering the way you perceive it. The way you might experience this is that people who used to irritate you don't press your buttons anymore, doom and gloom news reports of global recession don't stop you from pursuing new business ideas, and you perceive individuals as blessings whose former treatment of you caused you anger and bitterness.

Developing an attitude of detachment will help you to understand the nature of the pain you are experiencing. The vibration of detachment will help you to see the physical density of energy and to determine where the pain resides within you, how long the pain has been in existence, if the pain is yours or someone else's that you have taken on as your own, and also why you haven't yet let go of the pain. Numbness is a sign that you are carrying a large amount of pain in your body, mind, and spirit. The key to releasing pain effortlessly is allowing it to surface and transform into peace.

If you want to transform painful blocks, create space and a quiet time to do the following process. Begin by sitting with your eyes closed so that you can move into internal awareness. Take several deep breaths to increase sensitivity in your body. Use each breath to help you relax. If you feel any anxiety about doing this process, mentally reassure yourself that you are safe and all is well.

Next, sense, visualize, and feel your awareness beneath the soles of your feet. As you do this, you may feel the surface of your skin begin to tingle. This is a good sign. It means that you are already moving blocked energy.

Slowly move your awareness up through your body, half a foot to a foot at a time, in order to sense everything that is happening inside of you. You may experience hot and cold spots of energy, pins and needles, buzzing, twitching, a sensation like a light feather touching the surface of your skin, sudden sharp pain, dull aching, or tension, and you might feel as if your body is not big enough to fit comfortably inside your skin.

You will begin to feel intensity to these sensations, as your awareness of your internal energy increases. Stick with it and breathe through any discomfort you may feel. Your pain is rising to the surface and you are clearing it. That's all that means. This process is like putting steam on your face to prepare it for the extraction of blackheads. It feels uncomfortable when you squeeze impurities out of your pores, however your skin looks and feels great afterwards. Similarly you will find that you feel energetically clearer and lighter after undergoing this process.

As you spend a minute or so focusing your awareness on different parts of your body, ask yourself the following series of questions. Use these same questions every time you move to a new part of your body.

1. Where exactly am I feeling pain? You may hear, feel, or know the answer. If you are not conscious of receiving insights, trust that a shift is occurring within you. The answer will be revealed to you in perfect timing. The key here is to keep practicing to develop the ability to feel energy. Awareness is like a muscle that needs to be exercised.

2. How long has the pain been there? You may experience several layers of pain simultaneously or feel nothing at all. If you can't sense anything, bring your focus deeper inside of yourself.

3. Is this pain mine or is it someone else's pain, which I have absorbed? We are like sponges, absorbing energy all the time. Our energy fields are magnetic in nature. This is why it is imperative to develop awareness and to clear your electromagnetic field on a consistent basis.

4. If this pain is someone else's pain, whose pain is it? Often we take on other people's pain because we want to be sympathetic.

5. Why did I take this person's pain on? The answer to this question is telling. It will reveal unconscious energy patterns that are operating in your life. New awareness of these can help shift poor habits and challenges in setting healthy boundaries.

6. What are the payoffs for staying in pain? Some part of you definitely believes there is a benefit to the pain or you wouldn't have it. Mentally note the perceived benefits of the pain.

You have the option of taking five minutes for this exercise, an hour, or however much time you would like to develop deeper awareness of your energy field. The longer you take in doing the exercise, the more your awareness will intensify. If you choose to spend an hour on this practice, you could scan the energy in your entire body several times. If you are focused, on each successive round of scanning you will notice things you didn't spot before. Here are the body checkpoints to focus on:

- Half a foot below the soles of the feet and inside the feet

- The ankles, calves, shins, knees, thighs, and hip joints

- The reproductive organs

- The internal organs, including: the stomach, the colon, the spleen, the pancreas, the gall bladder, the liver, the kidneys, the heart, the chest, and (for women) the breasts

- The length of the spine, starting from coccyx and moving up to the neck

- The throat

- The head, including: inside the mouth (teeth, jaw, and tongue), the nose, the ears, the eyes, the brain, the forehead, the top of the head, and half a foot above the head

- The shoulders, arms, elbows, forearms, wrists, hands, fingers, thumbs, and the area that exists a quarter of a foot beyond the fingertips

As you awaken greater awareness, do not worry if you feel nauseous, this is simply stuck energy releasing. Take deep breaths and send the breath to where you feel the nausea emanating. For an hour to several hours afterwards, you may experience increased sensitivity to touch and sound. This is normal when developing intuition.

When I receive a massage, I'm so sensitive to energy that my body flinches to signal when someone is directly inside my energy field. I can feel it when the massage therapist's hands are half a foot outside of my body and moving towards physical contact with my skin. Someone talking near me can sound like shouting, it feels like the voice is ringing and echoing inside my head. When my ability to hear energy is heightened, I can hear the faint ticking of a clock from the other side of the room as loud and clear as if it is inside my head. I literally feel the vibration of each tick. Thankfully, these sensations are only temporary signs of my body upgrading to enhanced sensitivity. Then I can enjoy the massage.

It is best to do this exercise when you have time afterwards to calmly assimilate the activation of your sixth sense. I do not recommend doing it before spending time among a crowd or going into a situation where you will have to communicate with a lot of people. It could cause you to absorb all the energy you just let go of, plus more. You need to be in a gentle, quiet environment, surrounded by sensitive-aware people. Your body will feel hypersensitive when your awareness expands to a new level. Eventually, you will not be impacted by such feelings when your sixth sense increases.

The first time I tried to do a triceps extension with five-pound weights, I could barely move my arm. Now five pounds is easy. It's exactly the same when you work out your energy. Until this point in time you've only been working with a fraction of your potential. Human potential is actually infinite.

You can learn to expand your sixth sense so that you can quickly sense stuck energy and release pain, once you have built a foundation of understanding your own energy. I recommend you track your experiences and progress in your intuition journal. Don't worry if you cannot understand everything that is happening. You are safe. Nothing bad will happen to you. However, please do not try to rush this process. It is best not to do it more than twice a week for the first month.

As you accelerate your internal healing process, the blocks that you have experienced will quickly unravel in your life. How this usually comes to pass is you are presented with challenging situations, such as having to address relationships that are not in harmony with your life professionally and personally. Remember that developing your awareness is a lifelong process.

There is an illusion in certain New Age communities that we can experience enlightenment in a heartbeat and everything will be perfect. The key to enlightenment is to develop the qualities of heart, spirit, and soul. Enlightenment is non-reaction and acceptance of all energy that exists within the universe. Enlightenment is to understand the truth of who you are. I've met those who say they are enlightened and everyone else is out of alignment. They focus on ascension, meaning leaving the body and not living on Earth. I disagree with their approach. Without acceptance of the energy of time-space, enlightenment cannot be experienced in every moment.

Your key to enlightenment is focusing on acceptance of all that is. Part of this acceptance may involve the practice of saying no. Many healers, spiritual teachers, and students of enlightenment experience emotional abuse and boundary violation. They think that to connect to God they have to be wide open to everyone. The result is periods of feeling drained, exhausted, and hypersensitive. It doesn't have to be this way. Just recognize your negative energy saturation point. This means knowing when to take time out to recharge your batteries before you deplete your reserves. If you keep functioning at full speed when you are low on energy, you are susceptible to getting ill.

The Advantage of Pain

As my intuition ramped up, I became hypersensitive to energy. I did my best to ignore the spiritual transformation happening inside of me, and it made me physically ill. The night before I got sick, I'd gone out clubbing at Subterranea in Notting Hill. Several of us were standing up on stage, dancing and talking next to the DJ booth. I'd always loved doing this, however that night something felt different. I felt empty. I looked out at the people partying on the dance floor and I could see their energy. I experienced it as a black hole. I felt lost and alone. I questioned who I was and my purpose. I realized I had no purpose. Several of us went back to my friend's apartment at about 2:00 A.M. to hang out. That's when I began to feel awful, like people's energy was closing in on me: creepy, yucky energy. I said my goodbyes, but no one really noticed.

I walked out into the cool night air and waited for a taxi. The emptiness I'd felt inside the club hours earlier now consumed me. Eventually a taxi's yellow light shone in the distance. All I wanted to do was switch off from myself. The next morning, I woke up with my skin covered in a rash, feeling sick as a dog, which led to throwing up. I had developed both chicken pox and a severe case of tonsillitis. My throat was constricted so that I couldn't speak or eat. I sat up several nights in a row unable to sleep and doing my best not to scratch my skin. I sat on the floor of my penthouse condo and tried to take my mind off of everything by watching TV. That didn't work. I was miserable.

I was ill for three weeks. No one would come and see me because I was contagious. My parents left food with the security guard downstairs. My four cell phones stopped ringing because I was away from my job of doing the guest lists for the clubs. Soon I felt abandoned and helpless. Because I was insecure I began to question my friendships and the life I was leading. I made other people wrong. I thought they didn't care. Of course, that wasn't the case. It was my oversensitivity to the pain I was feeling.

The ultimate benefit of the pain was that I became a kinder, more compassionate person. But first I unknowingly became self-righteous. As my connection to spirit opened wide I became judgmental of my friends. I was so frightened of revealing who I really was that I rejected them before they could make fun of me. This was a mistake. I didn't understand the power of energy and thoughts. I didn't realize that there are rules in the spirit world, and one of these is that what you put out will come back to you.

When I began to have increased clairvoyance I easily panicked. At night, I'd see energy vibrating in the dark, like when you see the grey dots on a static TV screen. I remember the first time I saw all my furniture lose its density and become pure energy. Everything merged into one big light. I rubbed my eyes and shook my head, then ran out of my condo in the middle of the night. I was terrified. Another time, I stood in front of the bathroom mirror and watched myself turn into dots of energy and disappear.

I phoned Wendy, my mentor at the time, and told her about the crazy things that were happening to me. She reassured me they were perfectly normal. Wendy had been dressmaker to the Queen Mother and was married to a computer programmer. Wendy helped me understand what was happening to me. She had gone through the same transition as I. We talked on the phone for hours and she taught me all about ascended masters, angels, and guides. These are all beings that give wise benevolent guidance.

Ascended masters are spiritually enlightened beings. Ordinary humans in past incarnations, since then they have undergone a process of spiritual transformation. Angels act as guardians and messengers to guide you to best action. They may bring their essence into human form although their true appearance is as an emanation of light. Spirit guides usually are people who lived a previous life as a doctor or teacher in any number of professions or field of knowledge who now reside in a higher dimension. They are also beings from civilizations that exist in other dimensions. It is rare for a loved one to be your spirit guide, although loved ones may act as our guardian angels. A spirit guide will give many teachings to you once you are connected to their guidance.

Wendy also taught me a channeling technique that involved automatic writing. Channeling is allowing intelligent energy to move into your consciousness and give you guidance. Some people think they are channeling, but they're mistaken. True channeling only brings through positive guidance. Automatic writing is when you write without consciously thinking about what you are writing. It is stream of consciousness that flows through you to give higher guidance. After I'd written a channeled entry, I'd call her excited and wanting to understand what it meant. Every time she knew. Her response confirmed to me that I wasn't going nuts.

My Dad teased me when I told him I had channeled another message from Archangel Michael. I was excited but I also took myself a little too seriously. Of course, if someone had come up to me just a few years earlier and said he was channeling Archangel Michael and had a message, I'd have found it a little weird, too. Often my mom would call me eccentric. "Well at least I'm not boring," I'd say defensively.

Looking back, I can see that I was a pain in the ass. I thought I knew what was best for everyone. Oftentimes when I've channeled spirit guides or angels, I've felt like I'm making it up. However I've had too many experiences that confirm to me there is a world beyond our eyes to dismiss their messages. I'll talk about channeling in detail in the next chapter. For now, I'd like to share just one experience I had in January 2008 that once again confirmed to me that there are unseen helpers in a realm beyond ours.

For two months I had been receiving spiritual guidance from an ascended master called Saint Germain. He was teaching me how to give more effective psychic readings and guiding me in clearing my clients' stuck energy. I felt so silly at times. I'd think to myself, "If people only knew what is happening!" One day at the Aura Shop in Santa Monica, California, a book caught my eye: *So You Want to Be A Medium?* by Rose Vanden Eynden. I was compelled to read it within twenty-four hours. Right after I completed it, I heard a voice tell me, "The medium has a message for you." I was surprised to hear this because 95 percent of the time psychics can't read me. Nonetheless, I immediately scheduled a reading with the author Rose.

Rose didn't know anything about me before she did her reading. The first thing she said was, "You're surrounded in violet light and Saint Germain is with you." This was a powerful confirmation. For the previous seven weeks I'd been doing violet flame meditations every day and using the prayers of Saint Germain to strengthen my intuition. For the next 28 minutes of the reading, none of my questions were answered. I began to question whether or not Rose was a good psychic medium. Then I heard Saint Germain say, "Rose told you everything you needed to know. You don't need any other answers." I felt my body relax because I knew this to be true. I empathize with psychic mediums that are following spirit's guidance. My ego momentarily got in the way by wanting answers, as is often the case when someone is in pain during a psychic reading.

Whenever I've experienced pain, I know it is an indication that I'm in denial, disconnected, or ignorant. Pain tells me when I'm out of balance and it reminds me to take care of myself. Pain reveals when I'm having unconscious negative thoughts and it reminds me when my boundaries are not being kept in place.

Pain is purely a distortion in the energy field. If you feel it, it is telling you that you are going against your flow. You need to learn to interpret its message.

Your Pain Has a Specific Message For You

The best way to address pain is to feel it fully, rather than try to become more desensitized to it. Your pain has a specific message for you. When you understand why you have the pain, you can take a remedial action that will propel you forward to peace and fulfillment. As pain is activated in your body, your reflex is for your spirit to lift out of your body. It is the ego mind aspect of you that expels your spirit.

The way the energy looks from a clairvoyant perspective is that your energy is stretched outside of your physical body and your internal energy in your body is diluted and weakened. Taking deep breaths in through the nose and exhaling out through the mouth will assist you in directing the energy back into your body. Pain leaves your body when you have acknowledged it and you have accepted the message it has for you.

Three Simple Intuitive Techniques for Releasing Pain

A great benefit of becoming increasingly aware of your energy is that you will be able to ward off illness and pain. You won't be affected by depression or lethargy. You'll find that you require less sleep because situations that felt like major problems in the past now feel like minor matters that are easily addressed. Intense negativity disappears since intuition helps you perceive pain in a whole new light.

As you master your intuition, you'll be able to feel pain and be detached from it simultaneously. Your intuition at its best operates on multiple levels of awareness in many spatial realities while you live your daily life. It is important to keep yourself grounded as you open up to using your intuition to remove pain.

Use the following three visualization techniques to help you heal pain. At first you may feel like nothing is happening while you are doing these simple exercises. As you become more intuitive, you will sense the pain moving out of you.

Visualization #1: Waterfall of Light

This process transforms stuck energy into positive action steps.

Begin by sitting with your feet placed firmly on the floor. Ensure that your hands and legs are uncrossed to maximize the flow of your energy. Bring awareness to the soles of your feet to help you ground. As you breathe, feel your feet locking into the ground.

Then, move your awareness up through your body to the top of your head. Take both your hands, place them on top of your head, and push down on it in order to bring your focus into your body.

Next, visualize that you are sitting beneath a waterfall made of white light. Allow the energy to wash over you, cleansing your aura. Imagine the white light flowing through you and permeating every cell of your being. If the energy becomes too intense, inhale though the nose and out through the mouth several times. Then go back to your natural breathing pattern. This will help you stick with the visualization.

See if you can do this visualization for a full five minutes. It will strengthen your sixth sense and clear your body of unconscious patterns, locked inside of you.

Visualization #2: Pain Identity

The purpose of this exercise is to develop sufficient awareness to recognize buried pain. Often pain resides in layers deep inside of you. You won't necessarily be aware of it, however it will cause problems in your life that you won't consciously understand.

Begin by sitting or lying in a quiet place with your eyes closed. Take a few deep breaths. As you do so, visualize each breath taking you further inside your body. All you need to do is observe, feel, and sense what is happening in your body. You don't need to do anything else, because as you become aware of the energy blockages in your body, solutions will pop into your consciousness to resolve the problem at hand. This is being in the flow. The more you practice, the easier and more powerful it will be.

Visualization #3: Heart Centering

This technique is great for soothing the heart and nervous system, especially when you're feeling emotional or mental pain.

Begin by sitting or lying down. Do your best to relax into your body. Breathe in. Then, as you exhale, sense the body releasing tension.

Next, bring your awareness into your heart. As you drop your awareness deeper into your chest, sense your energy expanding. At first, you may find it challenging to expand your energy because it is so used to being constricted. With practice, you will be able to feel your true feelings beneath the surface of the ego mind. This creates a natural mechanism for releasing pain from your body.

There are a multitude of other techniques you could practice, which I share in my Intuition Development System™. I've found that with more experience these deceptively simple visualizations are the most effective. With time, you will find what works best for you. That is the beauty of your intuition.

Chapter 6

A WORLD BEYOND OUR EYES:
Practicing Clairvoyance

"If you can dream it, you can do it." — *Walt Disney*

Unless you enter into the world of Hollywood, you can't guess what's happening behind scenes. The director, the cameraman, and the lighting technician are diligently working, yet we don't see them when we're watching a movie on screen. Eighty percent of the production is occurring beyond our perception while we're watching actors Brad Pitt and Angelina Jolie perform. And that is also how we experience our lives. There is a swirl of activity occurring beyond our conscious perception. Spirit guides are directing us, angels are production-coordinating us, unseen lighting technicians are setting the mood for each scene that unfolds in our lives, and the deceased are our audience. Its always so, even when we don't see it.

You always have access to seeing "behind scenes" spiritually. The first step is to open to the possibility of it. People travel from all over the world to take a shot at making it in Hollywood. Few succeed. The ones who do succeed often have blind faith. A part of them knows that even though they can't see what is happening, it is happening. They sense it. The same principle applies to developing clairvoyance. There are two beliefs it is helpful to embrace. First, believe that there is a world beyond our eyes. To skeptics I say, "You believe radio waves exist even though you can't see them." The spirit world is energy, sort of like radio waves. Second, believe that seeing this world is not reserved only for a privileged few. Everyone has access. If you are willing, open, and receptive to seeing what is invisible through the vision of your eyes, you'll experience clairvoyance.

I've taught many people how to perceive subtle energy. The reason why people find it hard to see clairvoyantly is that they think they have to see in one particular way. But the harder you push to see, the more you actually block your psychic vision. That is why I advocate meditation. It helps clear energy blocks and, with practice, it also relaxes you to the point where you have access to the normally unseen world.

Although I didn't understand the full extent of my ability until my early twenties, I've been clairvoyant since I was six. I mistakenly thought everyone saw what I saw. I made my parents leave my bedroom door open at night because I was overwhelmed by the energy I could see in the dark. I saw shapes move in the room and I was terrified to put my feet on the carpet because I thought someone would grab my ankle from under my bed. Eventually, my parents insisted on closing the door. From then on, I'd sit bolt upright and focus on the sliver of golden light shining at the bottom of the door.

Sometimes I sat awake in the dark in my bedroom for three hours unable to sleep because my ability to see the energy made me hypersensitive. Seeing it took me deep inside myself and I didn't like what I saw. At the time I felt there was a lot of darkness inside me and I didn't understand why it was there. I now know it was both old energy from my past lives and new energy I had absorbed from people in my current life.

I don't believe it is a coincidence that children fear being in the dark. Children are incredibly sensitive to the unseen world. Do you remember what you saw as a kid? What memories did you shut out because they scared you or you were taught not to believe?

If the unseen world were accepted, it wouldn't be a dark secret. You'd have learned about it at an early age and probably explored your abilities. It wouldn't seem accessible only to a special few. Being clairvoyant means you have heightened vision. It is a muscle you can train. Anyone can do it. You already are clairvoyant.

In this chapter, I'm going explain the wonderful benefits of clairvoyance and how it can support you in your everyday life. For me, I originally perceived it as a curse because I didn't know how to use it. Once I did, it became a beautiful gift.

I'm going to give you a simple exercise you can practice right now to open your clairvoyance. Many people have had immediate results when they do this. If you don't see what I'm about to share with you right away, that's okay. Don't give up. You just need to practice a little more. You can do this exercise once a day. And if you do, you will begin to see clairvoyantly, and with more and more clarity.

Candle Vision Exercise "Awakening Your Clairvoyance"

The best time to do this exercise is in the evening when it's dark. If you try it during the daytime, close the blinds or curtains, and turn off the lights, so you can see what you are about to see. Get a candle (ideally a white candle) that is at least a few inches tall. This exercise does not work well with a tea light candle because it does not have enough height. I like to place the candle on a coffee table and sit on the floor in front of it. You'll want to place the candle at eye level, directly in front of you.

Once you've lit the candle, take some deep breaths to center yourself. With a soft, slightly unfocused gaze, look into the flame. Keep your focus here. You should begin to see a thin aura of green or red, or both colors, surrounding the golden flame. The longer you gaze at the flame, the more pronounced these colors will become.

After you've gazed at the candle for about a minute, close your eyes. Place your hands over your eyes and forehead. This focuses your vision inwards. Bring your awareness to your third eye, which is a spot positioned between the eyebrows at the center of your forehead. As you do this, press your two little fingers into the third eye to activate and stimulate it. Then rest the pads of your fingers gently on your forehead to integrate the awakening of your sixth sense.

With your eyes closed, you will see a yellow ball of energy surrounded by an outline of pink against a backdrop of black in your mind's eye. You may see the energy float in your mind's eye.

After about thirty seconds, open your eyes. Now you will see the ball of energy turn indigo surrounded by violet. It will be floating around the room.

Now go back to the first step of the exercise and gaze into the candle again.

This exercise will strengthen your psychic vision. If you are doing it for the first time, limit your session to five minutes because you do not want to over-stimulate your eyes. No harm can come to you if you do it longer. The only possible side effect is to feel wired and edgy. You are also likely to have vivid dreams as you open your psychic pathway.

Another thing that can happen is the flame of the candle grows taller. I've seen a candle flame extend a foot high on several occasions. When the flame does this, it becomes very thin and the top few inches of the flame move up and down in a very controlled manner. If this happens to you, it means your spirit guides are communicating with you through the flame. Often spirit guides make their presence known through electrical objects like lights, TVs, radios, computers, and, yes, candles.

It is fun to do this exercise with a friend and ask if you are seeing the same things for confirmation of your clairvoyance.

Now look around the room you are in. Can you perceive the energy? Can you see any blocks of energy? Do you see colors and shapes?

If you are with a friend, you may be able to see your friend's aura, which is a band of light that forms a perimeter an inch to a foot thick around the body. The aura is energy connected to the life force of our bodies. If you can, what color do you see?

When you become skilled at seeing energy you will be able to see a person's light body. This is people's spiritual essence that overlays their physical body. It looks like a golden light that grows brighter the more you look at it, and extends several feet out from the body to the left and the right.

If I'm having a fun, relaxed dinner with a couple of friends, I can usually see their light bodies because we're all open and operating from our higher selves—we're having a spiritual connection. When I was still dating, I'd see my date's aura or his light body if I were on a positive, happy date. Be mindful, however, that it's usually not a good idea to say to a guy you don't know well, "Hey, I can see your light body," as he might find it a bit strange. Get to know him a little better first before revealing this information.

As you're developing your sixth sense, you will be more open to all types of energy. It's best to give yourself time to integrate this new skill before sharing details about it. Once you've got it down, then, if it feels right, you can freely talk about it.

Some guys I dated when I was single loved it when I shared what I could see, whether that was the aura or the light body. We'd talk for hours about the spiritual realm. Others were freaked out and steered clear of me when I would bump into them later in one of the nightclubs. Today I know that they flipped out because they knew I could see them for who they really were. Guys who come off as super confident are often the most insecure about clairvoyance. But men with true self-confidence are strong, centered, and kind, like my husband Nick, and they don't get freaked out so easily. When I tell Nick I can see his aura, he teases me by ducking his head and looking furtively around the room.

Don't take yourself seriously or get offended if the person with whom you share the details of what you are seeing does not say, "Wow, that's so amazing." Focus on you and your experience. You're not responsible for another person's spiritual development. Each person gets to choose his or her own destiny.

If you're interested in developing stronger clairvoyance, there are numerous exercises you can practice, which I share in my home study course, The Intuition Development System™.

What to Look Out for

Being able to see raw energy, like you did using the exercise above, is the first step in developing clairvoyance. There are many other things you can see with your sixth sense in addition to raw energy. There is a misconception that being clairvoyant means you can see a dead person or an angel standing in front of you in Technicolor. In fact, this is a rare experience. It takes a large amount of energy for an entity in another realm to pronounce itself physically in this realm, because it has a different density than ours. Even if a dark energy is heavier than our own, in this dimension it will look physically paler because it exists on a different plane of consciousness.

A powerful form of clairvoyance occurs within the dream state. Have you ever seen a dead relative in a dream, had a conversation with him or her, and felt it was real?

It was. The reason why our spirit guides and loved ones who have passed over often communicate to us while we sleep is that we are more receptive in this state. The ego mind is resting so there aren't layers of mental objections to penetrate.

Another form of clairvoyance is *claircognizance*, which is seeing through knowing, as you would if you were blindfolded or physically blind. Basically, this is like having an overlay of an invisible picture on the world. You have an impression of a spirit guide—through knowing—and it is invisible to the naked eye, yet you perceive it as a visual image. With claircognizance,

I could see a man of forty with curly brown hair wearing a smoking jacket standing to the left of a client waiting to deliver a message. He's not physically there, but in my mind he's as plain to see as the table before me.

Spirit connected me with Heidi Hockman, an awesome woman who hosts an online community for people who are losing their eyesight or who have gone blind called **www.EverythingBlind.com**. I became friends with Heidi after a series of four dreams about going blind. I woke up from those dreams shaken, knowing spirit was showing me something related to keeping a check on my ignorance. It is easy to go blind from a mental, emotional, and spiritual standpoint. Because we see doesn't mean we are not blind in other ways. These dreams were a catalyst for me to deeply investigate my blind spots. We all have blind spots. Anyone who thinks they don't is in denial.

When I awoke from the first dream, I heard a voice clearly say, "Call Heidi." I phoned her right away. "Heidi, this may sound a little strange, but I'm going to say it anyway," I told her. "God told me to call you and that it's important."

"Doesn't sound strange to me. I prayed to God that someone would help me get the word out about Everythingblind.com and here you are," Heidi said.

I shared the details of my dream and what it felt like to go blind. Heidi confirmed that she had similar experiences when she lost her sight four years earlier to diabetes.

"We've got to do a teleseminar on blind spots. I must interview you," I said.

Weeks went by and I still hadn't committed to a date. Then I had three more dreams of going blind, two in one day, and another the following day. "I get it, I'll confirm a date now," I said to my spirit guides.

"How about doing a teleseminar on April 22?" I said.

"That's going to be my 40th birthday," Heidi said. To me, this was confirmation that both Heidi and myself are being supported by spirit. You know that expression, "Life beings at 40"? I believe that this was the birth of a new way of seeing for me. This is when I began to experience magic in my life in a whole new way.

When clients ask me to read their energy to see what's keeping them stuck or to tell them their probable futures, I find it easier to see when I close my eyes because it shuts out external stimuli and helps me zone in on the energy source, rather than on what is overlaying it. Surface energy creates distortions in our reality. Heidi confirmed to me that her ability to see what she needs to do in life is so much clearer now that she is blind.

You have the opportunity to see beyond your regular state of perception. If you commit to seeing from a new clairvoyant standpoint, you will save yourself time and money. You'll be able to see the truth of someone's intentions and actions, maybe beyond what they themselves know to be true. Clairvoyance turns into the gift of healing once you have developed understanding beyond the physical. When you can see someone's thoughts, this creates the space for you to be compassionate and forgiving to that person, even if looks on the outside like he or she is being hurtful or selfish. You may gently help that person grow if you care for him or her, or you may chose to walk away if this is a person whose core values are not in alignment with yours.

Clairvoyance may be experienced as a series of images that you see in your mind's eye. You could feel like you are imagining them, because you cannot physically see them. If you want to become an excellent clairvoyant, and perhaps even work professionally down the road as an intuitive, you will want to dedicate some space in your intuition journal to create a personal intuition dictionary. Record the images you see in it so that you can refer back to them later on if you see the same imagery.

The problem with most dream dictionaries is that they only provide rigid definitions. These may help you to a point with your clairvoyance, but then they will get you stuck. For example, if you see the image of a bed in your third eye, a dream dictionary might say it means, "Rest." You could be missing a true message from your spirit guide or guardian angel if you accept this definition on face value. The image of a bed can have several different meanings. Which one is correct depends on the person, situation, and environment that it relates to.

This is why when I'm unsure about a clairvoyant image's meaning I'll also use my clairaudience and clairsentience to get as much confirmation as possible to ensure that I understand the intuitive guidance. I will explain more about clairaudience (hearing) and clairsentience (feeling) in the next two chapters. My point here is that I can get a clear visual image that could be interpreted in a couple of ways, so I make very sure not to jump to conclusions. I ask for more guidance that comes via the pathways of my other physical senses. I'll even be specific with my guides, "Could you give me an auditory confirmation of that, please?" Goose bumps and shivers are also signs of confirmation.

Another form of clairvoyance is seeing photographic images in the third eye. A couple of months ago, Nick and I were at home watching TV on a Saturday night and the movie *Next,* starring Nicholas Cage, was on. I'm a big fan of Cage, but this movie was ridiculous in terms of how it represented clairvoyance. There was a scene where Cage knows a bullet is going to be fired at him and he dodges it because he had a flash of it happening a split second beforehand. Oh please!

Clairvoyance is much more ordinary than that. You are most likely to see photographic images in your mind's eye when you are meditating or receiving a healing modality like Reiki or Shen. You can see the image because the activity of meditation or healing unlocks a memory held in your body at a cellular level. The visual scenes you mostly likely will see are from past lives. They usually last no more than 90 seconds. This kind of seeing can happen whenever you are in an altered state of awareness.

You Can See Beyond What You Think Is Possible

You can experience all the forms of clairvoyance I described above. All you have to do is open your mind and your heart. Don't be so quick to judge the form information comes to you in or to dismiss your imagination. Stop being fixed in your thinking. Allow energy and situations to wash over you instead of trying to control them. Once you have developed the skill of clairvoyance, then you may practice controlling energy. This does not mean manipulating energy, it means mindfully and responsibly directing energy for a positive intention. The more you practice the easier it will get.

Your level of receptivity and your natural sensitivity to energy will determine how fast you are able to see unseen energy. As I mentioned before, I remember being clairvoyant since I was six, it took me decades to integrate this skill into my life. I went through many ups and downs. Sometimes my clairvoyance would be extremely powerful, however, if I fell in love with a guy who wasn't good for me, using clairvoyance on behalf of myself went out the window. Also if I got angry about a work situation, worried about money, or felt hurt by a friend, my inner guidance would falter. Fortunately I could still see clearly for others because I was emotionally detached from what they wanted.

The way I overcame my blocks to intuition was to commit to educating myself and trusting my intuition when I was feeling angry, resentful, critical, bitchy, sorry for myself, or depressed. I learned that the only way to get clear guidance was first to affirm to myself, "I am not my emotions," and then to determine if the feelings in my body were mine or someone else's. When I let myself feel why I had these negative emotions, when I dropped deep inside the emotions, they would transform into peaceful energy. Sometimes it would feel as if my body was being turned inside out as this transformation occurred, however a part of my soul knew that all would be well. I trusted this pain because I knew it would pass. It always did and was replaced by a newfound clarity that supported me in manifesting what I wanted in my life.

Realistically you can develop a solid foundation of trusting your clairvoyance in a year. If you practice intuition techniques daily, you may receive many signs of progress within the first month to three months, however you'll likely go through some bumpy periods as you clear out the old blocks and integrate new energy. Stick with it, because it'll help you improve every area of your life.

Clairvoyance with Benefits

The biggest benefit of clairvoyance is being able to create the outcomes that you want in your life. Of course you do not have control over others' decisions, but you can develop confidence in every action step you take. Clairvoyance helps you see the truth of a situation. It eliminates doubt, because you can see what is really happening. Wouldn't it be great to know that starting your new business is a good idea? Or have confirmation that doing a joint venture with someone will be prosperous for you both? You can eliminate stress and worry with clairvoyance, as you're not going to get any surprises. You've analyzed and investigated the energy, to confirm it's a clear path to success.

On the other hand, what if you look at a situation that looks great on the surface yet your clairvoyance shows you otherwise? One of my clients wanted guidance about a too-good-to-be true business opportunity. He had been struggling to keep his company afloat and someone was offering a nice-sized investment to have partial ownership in his business. On the surface, it looked like this investor was the cream of the crop and could help leverage my client's situation, saving him time and money. I closed my eyes while on the phone with him and tapped into the energy of this potential investor. Yuck.

This potential investor was a snake. He wanted to include my client's business in another deal to stop my client's business from competing with one he'd already raised financing for. This would have brought my client's business to a grinding halt. My client had already invested $500,000 into his business and a year of his time, and this potential investor wanted 51 percent ownership. "You've got free will but if I was you, I wouldn't do it. This man's intentions are not pure," I said.

My client was exasperated. "But I need the money. What if another investor doesn't come along?" he asked.

"What if your $500,000 gets stuck in this deal and you're in a holding pattern because your new partner calls the shots?" I said.

"I'm scared. What if this doesn't work out?" he said.

"It will work out if you hang in there. Go find another investor. Get on the phone right after you get off the phone with me and you'll find someone," I said.

Two weeks later my client called me for another session. "You were right. We did some due diligence on this guy and he totally had his own agenda. Oh, good news, we found another investor. It's not as much money as we'd like to have, but it's enough to get us to the next phase. We've still got control of our business," he said.

As you can see the skill of clairvoyance can save you a lot of money.

When I was hosting a psychic TV show in the UK, I used to get asked all the time, "Can you give me the lottery numbers?" My answer is no. Clairvoyance is a skill and gift to be used for the evolution of your soul, not for laziness, personal greed, or ego. Looking for a quick way to make a lot of money will lead you down the wrong path, and spirit guides and guardian angels will play no hand in that game.

If you want to make big bucks, your clairvoyance can identify your hidden skills and ideas that when implemented will bring you super-success. The key is that you have to take action with the information you receive. Receiving clarity that you are a great singer does not mean becoming a Grammy award-winning singer. These are two different outcomes. What do you want? Are you willing to take the necessary steps to get those exact results? It's up to you to follow through on the guidance you have received.

When I received clear inner guidance fifteen years ago that part of my purpose and achievement in life involved being a best-selling author, it didn't happen. For the first few years I wondered why it hadn't happened. I thought I'd randomly meet an agent or publisher at a party, who would turn and say to me, "You're so interesting. I'm impressed by your knowledge. I want you to write a book and we'll publish it for you." How naïve. I knew a fraction then of what I know now about intuition. It was repeated clairvoyance that gave me the will and encouragement to hone my skills. I did over a thousand psychic readings, attended many writing courses, and wrote in my journal almost every day for twelve years. I wrote a book and a screenplay before I finally wrote what you have in your hands. Being psychic is not enough. Following your intuition is what you have to do if you want to create the success you know you're meant to have happen.

Clairvoyance can help you a great deal in love. When I've done psychic readings, I've repeatedly seen clients misconstrue their boyfriends' or ex-boyfriends' intentions. My clients felt extreme pain and low self-esteem, as they held strong to this belief. They couldn't move on and they couldn't let go. They were emotionally stuck. When I showed them what the ex or current boyfriend's actions meant, they're hearts melted. The unattractive ice-cold defense disappeared and they felt like a weight had been lifted. As a result they either had a positive breakthrough with intimacy in their current relationship or they developed the courage to move on effortlessly, and shortly after meet someone else. Clairvoyance can support you in making the right choices for your heart.

I put myself through much pain and humiliation because I didn't listen to my intuition. Every time I ignored it, I got really hurt. I'd always blame the guy and call him a "bastard." It was never his fault. I put myself in those painful situations every time. A gun wasn't held to my head. I didn't know that the pain of being sexually abused at age 11 by my best friend's godfather had impacted me at a deep level. I put myself in scary situations with boys throughout my teenage years, where I felt violated. As years went by, I solidified an unconscious pattern of having no clear boundaries with men.

Your clairvoyance is an opportunity to unearth your pain. The thoughts I finally extracted were that I was "dirty" and "didn't deserve love." Repeatedly facing the dark places inside myself released these wounds and energy blocks from my life. I encourage you to be courageous and look inside yourself. You may be surprised by what you find.

Be gentle with yourself. As your clairvoyance develops, areas where you have been in denial will come to conscious awareness for healing. It is not a good idea to rush your process of internal discovery. As you become aware of the truth about certain relationships in your life, a lot of uncomfortable energy can come rushing to the surface. Sit with the energy for a little while before communicating how you feel to the involved party. If you feel the impulse to talk with someone immediately, this is your pain and ego doing the guiding. It is important that you focus on clearing your energy and resolution from a standpoint of healing not of blaming or antagonizing. If the person involved pushes energy on you, explain that you need more time. If you can't listen without getting angry, definitely delay the communication. Remember, everything has its perfect timing. Your clairvoyance will help you to see that perfect timing.

If you realize it's time to leave your current job, don't rush into impulsive action or sabotage yourself in the workplace. I've seen many people do that. Integrate your realization so that you take every new action from a state of awareness and confidence rather than a state of fear and frustration.

Spirit is constantly encouraging us to grow. If we stay in a situation that we are not learning from, the job or the relationship we're in will become increasingly difficult. Why get fired or dumped? Leave with grace. Have faith and you will be guided to the best opportunities sooner than you may anticipate.

The Purpose of Clairvoyance

The purpose of inner vision is to guide you to understand and embrace your life's purpose. Are you aware of your life purpose? Are you living it? How would you feel if today was your last day on Earth? Have you done the best you can to live the life your soul wants to experience? Clairvoyance gives you the ability to see pure truth.

Some people do not want to experience clairvoyance because then they would have to confront their denial. Are you ready to see the whole truth? It can be painful when you see how people really feel about you. Compromising your heart will leave it heavy. So I encourage you to let go of excuses. You will not regret awakening your sixth sense because the rewards of intuition far outweigh the pain you may experience. As you release the blocks from your life that are holding you back from your fullest potential, your energy will become lighter and you will develop a profound inner strength.

You may wonder why some people have highly developed clairvoyance while others do not. Everyone has the ability of clairvoyance within, except it lies dormant in some of us. It is up to you to awaken your intuition. It is your free will. No one can make you do it. In my own life, for a period I tried to shut my intuition down. I resisted delivering the messages I was shown and told by spirit guides for fear of responsibility and not wanting to be criticized. Yet I knew that my life purpose was to show people how to awaken their intuition. My spirit guides told me quite bluntly to get over it. "You say you want to be of service to humanity. Well, here's how you can help," my guides said.

If you practice following your own intuition, you'll know what to do. You will see the world from an entirely new perspective. Things that bothered you before won't upset you anymore. At times you will have painful realizations as you allow yourself to be vulnerable to clairvoyance. The path of the Sixth Sense is not all airy-fairy and perfect. It can tough. But you will feel the most alive you've ever felt in your life if you allow spirit to enter into your life.

You can take the first step right now on to the road of clairvoyance. Ignite the belief that it is possible to expand your perception of what you see. Take time in the evening to soften your gaze as you sit in your bedroom before sleep. This will open you up to clairvoyance through your dreams. Look around you. What can you see?

As you develop your sensitivity to enhanced sight, you may feel butterflies in the solar plexus. This is normal and shall pass, as the energy settles. You won't see anything you cannot handle. Your spirit guides are benevolent and want what's best for you.

What You Can Expect from Clairvoyance

You will have days on which your ability to see energy is heightened, and at other times you will feel like nothing is happening. Be patient with your progress if you are a beginner. As I went through my own development I had periods of accelerated growth, and then suddenly it would feel like my ability to see had shut down. Later I learned that my body was integrating new energy that I had awakened. I was not disconnected. My spirit guides were just protecting me from being over-sensitive to my circumstances.

If you feel like you are experiencing disconnection enjoy the downtime. When your sensitivity ramps back up you'll need to focus to ensure you gain clarity. As you fine-tune your skill of clairvoyance, you will build your own intuition dictionary for communication with your spirit guides and guardian angels.

Chapter 7

HELLO, CAN YOU HEAR ME?
Practicing Clairaudience

"So when you are listening to somebody, completely, attentively, then you are listening not only to the words, but also to the feeling of what is being conveyed, to the whole of it, not part of it."
—Jiddu Krishnamurti

It took me years to realize that my guardian angel was speaking to me. I was surprised when a voice in my head suggested actions that were wise and sensible. Where was this wisdom coming from? Did I follow its lead? Oftentimes no. Did I wish I had? Duh. Only a guardian angel could be this patient. My parents weren't. I don't blame them.

You are often being given guidance, however you are not aware of it. Here's another misconception: People think they have to hear their spirit guides in Dolby Stereo, booming like the voice of God. When I've received God's guidance, I've had to listen carefully for it. It is usually quiet and firm and, of course, filled with love. As I dived into fascination with the psychic world in my early twenties, I learned about one modality of the sixth sense, *clairaudience*, in a psychic development course. It was like a dam had burst open and every conceivable sound you could hear came rushing and gushing into my head.

Guardian Angels, Spirit Guides, and Your Higher Self

As I opened to the ability to hear sounds beyond my regular perception, often I was distracted and ungrounded. I was so focused on the sounds and voices in the other realm that I wasn't capable of listening to what people were saying. Have you ever had a conversation with someone who seems like they are distant and daydreamy? You know, like they're in Seventh Heaven after great sex? That's how I was. I felt like I was having a love affair with clairaudience. I was constantly fascinated by what I could hear. I found it most entertaining. I got caught up in the sensationalism of the "Isn't this cool" of clairaudience, instead of listening and acting upon the wise guidance.

My best friend at the time Mark was attending psychic development classes with me. We got into competition with each other about who was hearing better stuff and receiving stronger guidance. We were both insecure and needed to prove ourselves.

Looking back it wasn't the wisest thing to do when I was having dinner with my family or a date and said, "Archangel Michael thinks you need to do X, Y, or Z." Psychics often use the excuse of channeling a spirit guide or angel to tell people what to do without taking any responsibility for their own words. The psychics that do this are the ones who are all in ego and want to be top dog. I remember being in Egypt with fourteen psychics traveling down The Nile in a boat and a huge argument broke out.

"My channeling is better than your channeling. Where are you getting your channeling from anyway?" Psychic #1 said.

"It's coming from Metatron," Psychic #2 said.

"Well I'm talking directly with God and he says that you need to listen to me now or you won't ascend," Psychic #1 said.

"Ashtar Command must speak, Ashtar Command must speak, behold, behold, if you do not listen you will die," Psychic #3 said.

The thing is that there were moments when all three of these psychics were tapped into source and did receive good guidance. But when their egos kicked in, the scene turned into a ridiculous farce. Psychic #3 got so pissed that he wasn't being listened to, he pretended to collapse on the floor to get all attention focused on him. When he sensed everyone's eyes were on him, he launched into channeling, yet acted like he was unconscious. Afterwards when he "regained consciousness," he claimed not to remember a word he said to validate that indeed the message was from Ashtar's Command.

This sort of malarkey goes on in the New Age community all the time. I encourage you to look past this and instead to focus on developing your ability to hear from a heightened state of perception. Learn from my mistakes and don't get caught up in sensationalism. There are some genuine psychic mediums out there, like Reverend Juliet Nightingale, who communicate with the deceased and spirit guides. Don't let other crazy psychics and scam artists put you off from developing your clairaudience. Psychic sensationalism is all the more reason for you to develop your own skill.

I want to make you aware of the different types of clairaudience you could experience. This will help you attune to the subtle energies of what you don't normally hear. Bats, dogs, and cats are examples of animals that have a heightened perception of sound. My dog Winston barks way before I hear someone arrive at our house. He can always tell if it's Nick or a stranger arriving without seeing who is there. In fact, all my pets are congregated together to greet me when I walk in the front door to my home.

Someone who is blind has to rely on his or her ability to hear for guidance. They can sense the height of a person, where a person is positioned in a room, and understand the mood the person is in based on subtle sounds like breath and movement. Clairaudience can help you know when your guardian angel or spirit guides are in your presence so you can get ready to receive higher guidance. Good clairaudience is like getting free coaching from an expert in your field of interest. You have this skill.

If you haven't communicated with a spirit guide or your guardian angel before, the being will more likely converse with you while you sleep, because your receptivity is better in that state. Have you ever woken up from a dream and felt a strong urge to call someone or take a specific action? You've probably received clairaudient guidance through your subconscious mind. Your guides may work with you like this for a time while you increase your ability to be able to hear communication. How clogged up your head is with thoughts and worries determines how quickly you can learn to hear intuitive guidance.

Not everyone has a guardian angel. I've worked with a couple of clients where when I've called upon their guardian angels no one has showed up. In these cases, I've made a request for the best possible match to support my client. A guardian angel always appears. Clients will ask if they'd done something bad that caused them not to have a guardian angel. Of course not! At birth, the clients may have been overlooked.

Angels can make mistakes, although only on rare occasions. However, they're quick to admit it when they have and they come up with a solution super-fast.

Let's clarify the differences between your guardian angel, spirit guides, and higher self. This will help you recognize where the guidance is coming from. First, your guardian angel is constantly by your side from the point of your conception onwards and is protecting you from harm throughout your life. Second, spirit guides work with you in an educational capacity and help you to integrate life lessons. You may have more than one spirit guide at a time and your guides may change during your lifespan depending on your soul's growth and requirements, and because you have free will. Third, your higher self is the wisest part of your soul. It is the source of the driving desire of your spirit to create harmony.

Here's an opportunity for you to open up communication with your guardian angel. This is a good place to start. You can repeat the same steps I'm about to show you to begin a conversation with your higher self or your spirit guides. As you become adept at communicating beyond your regular state of perception, you'll be able to hear guidance from your guardian angel, higher self, and spirit guides all at once. But initially it is best to break down the process into smaller pieces so you do not miss subtle energy.

Guardian Angel Communication Exercise

Sit in a position that feels comfortable to you. Place your feet firmly on the floor to ground your energy and your hands in your lap, palms facing upwards (amplifying your receptivity to energy). Ensure that your spine is straight. You may also opt for a cross-legged position. Do whatever feels best for your body. Listen to what your body needs to be able to open the channels of communication.

Then, take several deep breaths in through the nose and out through the mouth. As you do this, relax your shoulders away from your ears and sense the energy around your chest releasing and opening.

Now drop your awareness into your belly and again take several deep breaths in through the nose and out through the mouth. As you do this, become aware of the blocks and limitations that stop you from hearing clear guidance. Use your breath to guide you deeper inside yourself.

Notice the sounds around you. Can you hear energy moving? Subtle energy often sounds like a gushing stream. You may hear a ringing in one of your ears for a few seconds. This is confirmation that you have connected to the frequency of your guardian angel, meaning you can receive a message from the angel without physically hearing it. This aspect of clairaudience is pure knowing of what you are hearing (claircognizance) and it is equally as effective as consciously hearing guidance. You simply experience a strong knowing inside of you.

Understanding Clairaudience

The reason you may not hear the information that's being spoken as being spoken aloud is twofold. First, your vibration is not high enough yet to tune in and, second, it is not necessary to hear all guidance in words. It may be given as pure energy with a more powerful result because negative patterns or habits can be removed at a cellular level.

If you do hear a voice speaking, it is likely to sound like your own voice in your head, and only very rarely like a voice from outside of you. The time when you may hear an external voice is when a group of spirit guides is present to support you. You will have to extend your focus several feet away from you in order to hear them, as they will not infringe upon your space.

When I began having the types of experiences described above, it took me many years to understand what was happening. I meditated and did many intuitive readings to decipher the meaning of each sensation. Developing your own understanding will help you remove barriers to experiencing your sixth sense.

Remember, you are safe and your guardian angel will always be gentle with you when it communicates, even if it is firm. Consider your guardian angel as a wise, loving parent who only wants what is best for you. Many of my clients have voiced the fear, "How do I know if what I'm hearing is really coming from my guardian angel?" If guidance makes you fearful instead of aware, it's not coming from a loving place.

The more you practice listening for guidance, the easier it will be to determine whether the guidance you receive is coming from your ego mind or the wise loving part of you, your higher self, a spirit guide, or a guardian angel.

When you are sitting in a state of inner awareness, you may also feel a fluttering or tickling inside of your eardrums. This confirms that you are attuning to a higher wave of communication.

Here's what to look out for that will confirm to you when intuitive guidance is coming from a lower realm: the voice is outside of you and it will whisper in your ear. It will try to put fear in you by telling you that something bad will happen to you if you don't follow the guidance. This is the voice of a negative entity or lost soul, who has no power over you. These beings only have power if you fear them. Remember, you do not need to listen to them. They need you, but you don't need them. They hook into people by tapping into their fears. If you ever have this experience, remind yourself, "My fears have no power over me." Even if you feel scared, repeating this affirmation several times sends a positive action to the unconscious mind. Nothing bad can happen to you.

Rest assured, hearing a negative entity or having an encounter with one is highly unlikely to happen. However, it is best to be aware so that you can nip it in the bud before it tries to communicate with you. As I began to develop my sixth sense, I found it so exciting that I left myself wide open to anything and everything most of the time. I later learned this wasn't a good idea. I was ungrounded, over-sensitive, and caught in pride that "I can hear spirit," rather than wondering, "What is spirit communicating to me? Is it good guidance? Can I trust what I'm hearing?"

A few months ago, I had to carry out an exorcism for one of my clients. I've never experienced anything like this before in my life. I know it happened because I was ready to tackle this sort of situation. Your guardian angel and spirit guides would never put you in a situation that you were not ready to handle. I have to admit, I was a little bit nervous before doing the session. I knew it would be an exorcism because, as I took my client through a guided meditation, I saw her soul lift out of her physical body and a dark force began to speak through her. I found out later on that she had no recollection of it.

The way I knew with absolute certainty that I had exorcised a lost soul was that my client told me it was the angel who sits on the right hand of God whispering in her ear. Angels don't whisper in your ear or give you commands. The energy of this entity felt sinister. If you ever feel intimidated by spirit, that spirit does not have your best interests at heart. You have free choice as to what actions you take in your life.

I knew I would have to prepare myself mentally, emotionally, spiritually, and physically to clear this energy out of my client's life. We reconvened the next afternoon and I made sure I wore a cross. I am born Jewish, however, when it comes to clearing negative entities out of someone's energetic space, I always call upon Christ in addition to God's light. I repeated the Lord's Prayer over and over until I knew the entity had gone. What I discovered was that this spirit was a Benedictine monk who had dedicated his life to God. When he died, he felt cheated. If you pray to God with ulterior motive, you will never be fulfilled. The spirit of this man was remnant energy from one of my client's past lives. When someone carries a negative entity inside, it is usually an unresolved issue from a past life that is sitting in the aura. When it feels it is being pushed out, it moves to a different part of the person's energy field and resides there.

Transforming the entity's negative thought process was an intense experience. The spirit didn't was to leave because he feared he would be tricked and abandoned. It's the first time I've felt an entity really throw its energy at me in a highly threatening way. I reminded myself, "No harm can come to me. I am safe." I focused on pure love to move this spirit on. And move on he did.

This story describes a rare situation. But I want you to know that when a spirit guide says, "You must do this," "If you don't do this you will suffer," "She is evil," or "He is a bad person," it is not one of your spirit guides speaking. Just because a person is dead and communicates from beyond doesn't mean it is the best guidance for you.

I also wanted to share this information with you because you may know someone who is in a highly negative mindset. If this is so, it is likely they have a negative energy hooked into them. Affirmations and goal setting are wonderful mindset tools, however they only work on the mental plane. To create absolute fulfillment and peace in your life, it is not enough to focus only on the mind. What about body and spirit?

This stuff can seem a little woo-woo and crazy, but I've been in enough situations where I've done psychic medium readings for people whose loved ones have passed over and told them things I couldn't possibly know that I believe it. I have a pragmatic and skeptical side to me, so it feels weird writing about this stuff. But I know my experiences are true. My suggestion is to focus upon what feels good and supportive for you.

The time you are most likely to hear the voice of a deceased loved one or spirit is right before you fall asleep when your awareness is shifting from your conscious mind into a state of expanded perception. If you are already sensitive to energy and feel overwhelmed by it, you can put one of the following stones under your pillow or hold it in your hand before you go to sleep to keep you grounded and energized.

Crystals and Stones to Develop Your Intuition

- Rose quart will create a force field of love, gentleness, and peace around you.

- Black tourmaline will absorb the trillion unconscious thoughts you've had during your busy day and negativity, so you won't leave yourself open to unwanted energy.

- A river rock or pebble from the beach will ground, calm, and center your energy before and while you sleep.

- A gratitude rock, with a written affirmation or symbol on it, will help you set a specific field of intention around you before you go to sleep. A circle or a figure of eight are two excellent symbols that create support for your soul in the form of harmony, wholeness, and balance.

- Be aware that if you put a piece of labradorite or lapis lazuli under your pillow it will amplify your ability to hear your spirit guides. If you have a very practical nature and are grounded and pragmatic, these stones will work well for you.

- If you use a piece of clear crystal quartz, make sure you program it with a specific intention first before sleeping. To do this, hold the stone, close your eyes, and direct your intention into it: "I receive gentle supportive communication from my guardian angel and spirit guides while I sleep. I will remember what is important and relevant and know how to follow through on this guidance when I wake up."

- I'm a big fan of amethyst. This gemstone is restorative for the nervous system and heart. It will encourage the awakening of your sixth sense in a gentle, yet deep way and is the most effective stone for integrating the will of your higher self while you sleep.

Receiving Guidance from Your Higher Self

As you develop confidence in your sixth sense, you will find that it gets easier to receive guidance from the wisest part of your soul. Your higher self will guide you automatically without you needing to think about how to connect with it. You may have already experienced moments of this in your life. You can maintain this as an ongoing connection. A very effective way to strengthen the guidance from your higher self is to do a few minutes gentle meditation followed by journaling. Write down this question:

"What is my next best step regarding my relationship/career/finances?"

If you only listen to the guidance, you may feel like you're making in up. Writing it down creates space in your head for ideas to present themselves that you haven't thought of before. It can feel like a flash of insight or a positive command, one that you need to learn to act upon even if it doesn't seem rational and your ego mind protests. Often my higher self will tell me to call or write to someone specific or research a particular topic, or find a piece of information that leads me to fulfill my goal.

My favorite form of clairaudience is receiving guidance through music. Have you ever listened to a song on the radio and felt it was speaking to you?

Guardian angels and spirit guides love making you aware through music because a melody has a higher vibration than something that is only spoken. Music permeates the mind and spirit, and uplifts your energy in a way words alone do not. Why do movies have a soundtrack? *Jaws* wasn't a success with audiences until John Williams added the theme tune. Music works on the emotional body. You can hear one musical note and a whole message can be conveyed to you. When I hear a couple of notes of *Superman*, I feel like I can achieve anything. It gives me the energy to break through any unconscious limiting beliefs I may have. That's the power of music.

Sometimes I'll hear a line from a song repeating over and over in my head. I know that my guardian angel wants to bring my attention to a specific focus when this happens. If you want to know more details about your spirit guides, they may inform you through music. For example, hearing a sitar playing in your head could mean you have an Indian guide. Spirit can be very creative in their communication.

I encourage you to be patient with the skill of clairaudience. Some people have naturally developed it and for others it takes more effort to awaken it. Most people are predominantly clairsentient (you will read about this in the next chapter), clairvoyant, rather than being clairaudient. If your head is clogged with an excess of thoughts, it will be hard for you to receive clairaudient guidance until you've cleared enough space for active listening. Sit quietly, meditate, and exercise to clear your head.

How much you're spinning in your head or to what degree you are ungrounded is a determining factor in how long it takes for you to hear clear guidance. If you're open and receptive, and your mind is still, it can happen right away.

Everyone is born with a strong inner voice. It may be less well developed within people who were not given the opportunity to express themselves creatively or who grew up in homes where their perspectives weren't valued. A person who has experienced physical or sexual abuse usually shuts him or herself down for self-preservation. A part of the person knows he or she would have to take actions that feel overwhelming or too traumatic to follow through on. It can feel safer to go into denial than to act courageously. Sometimes, that is what needs to happen for a period of time to heal the internal wounds. Each person's soul has a perfect time for awakening to the sixth sense.

Benefits of Clairaudience

The great thing about clairaudience is that it's another way for you to confirm the intuitive messages you're getting through your other intuitive senses, like clairvoyance and clairsentience. It is great to feel confident about the guidance you are receiving and not to need to go to someone else for the answers you are seeking. You can share your wisdom and experiences instead of coming across needy and insecure. Clairaudience can open you to an improved understanding of yourself.

Clairaudience can protect you from harm. A participant in one of my workshops told me that when she was about to get in an elevator in Italy, an inner voice (her higher self) told her not to step in and instead to wait in the basement. The logical part of her mind thought this was totally irrational, however she followed her clairaudient guidance. It turns out that if she'd gone into the elevator, she would have been held at gunpoint and robbed along with the other unsuspecting civilians who rode it.

I remember one time I'd been given very clear inner guidance not to date a guy who seemed great. My friends told me I was crazy to turn him down. Soon afterwards I discovered he had four girls in rotation at once, telling each one he thought they were the best things ever. Your clairaudience can help you get beneath the surface of what's really going on. You can literally hear someone else's thoughts when you are attuned.

Another time, my intuition felt like it was screaming at me not to go into business with a seemingly spiritual woman. She had a good heart, however she had suffered much abuse in her life and unfortunately this led her be unreliable and passive-aggressive. Thankfully I only did a small amount of work with her and because of my clairaudience, I terminated our relationship quickly before any real damage to my business could occur.

Your first step in developing clairaudience is to practice active listening. This means becoming aware through your auditory perception of external and internal sounds. What do you really hear when someone speaks with you? Are you conscious of the subtexts of conversations? There are always subtexts to remain aware of. For example, when a man tells a woman, "I don't want to get in a committed relationship, I'm not ready," but then marries a different woman and has a baby with her months after, what was he really saying? His subtext was: "I don't want to commit to you."

A woman saying, "I accept you as you are," in truth could mean, "I really want you to change, but I don't think you will, so I have decided to suffer unhappiness."

The biggest cause of problems in my client's lives is miscommunication and misunderstanding. Clairaudience removes distortions in listening and thus creates clearer communication and excellent relationships. If you listen, you will hear the whispers of the wisdom that is always available for you revealing unspoken messages.

If you practice active listening for a month and journal your experiences, you'll find that your relationships improve considerably. Already good relationships will take on a new depth and meaning. You'll also have the courage to spend less time with people who are insincere and move on from manipulative and negative relationships. Eventually you'll know if people really mean what they're saying because you'll be able to read their energy clearly. Even if they may think they are being honest, they may not be clear about their thoughts and motivations. Clairaudience will help you see others' denial, allowing you to keep your heart open and to be compassionate despite their lack of awareness. This actually creates the space for you and them to grow spiritually.

The surer you are of yourself, the more inner peace will be yours. Keep listening and if you notice that you've disconnected from your inner voice, start again right away.

Chapter 8

IT HURTS SO MUCH AND IT FEELS SO GOOD:
Practicing Clairsentience

"Often you have to rely on intuition." —Bill Gates

Ever since I was a child, I've been extremely sensitive to people's feelings. I can feel it most acutely when people have numbed their pain and buried it in the unconscious mind. When people are hurting, my natural tendency is to want to take the pain away and rescue them. For me connecting with hurting men and trying to ease their pain became a form of addiction. People who are highly sensitive to energy are prone to addiction, because, among other things, they use their addictions to dull painful feelings they sense. If you can relate to this comment, you may be highly sensitive with an addictive personality. An addiction could be to chocolate or watching television, as easily as cocaine or alcohol. Everyone has his or her own way of finding comfort when life gets tough.

My past addictions were food and chasing after emotionally wounded men. My ability of *clairsentience,* meaning "clear feeling," always led me to create drama in my life and attract men who author Julia Cameron refers to in *The Artist's Way* as crazy makers. I rationalized that it was better to suffer a broken heart and all the physical and emotional pain that went along with it than to have smooth sailing without feeling. Part of me liked intense feelings of pain because they made me feel deeply alive.

For a long time, I set up an unconscious pattern for myself where I was so busy focusing on another person's pain and drama that I didn't have to face the issues that needed to be addressed in my life, like learning how to take responsibility for my actions. I hoped and dreamed that everything I wanted would miraculously fall into my lap with no effort. I grew up surrounded by some of the most beautiful, successful people in the world. I assumed that everyone hung out with celebrities and dated super models while eating $2,000 dinners, drinking Cristal champagne, and zooming around in Ferraris and Lamborghinis. Anything less than a five-star hotel or the latest Gucci shoes meant failure. In this setting, it was the norm to be at parties with people doing a lot of cocaine.

At nineteen, on vacation in the South of France at a stunning hillside villa one of the guys I was with poured a pile of cocaine the size of a small mountain onto a glass coffee table. As everyone except for me started to snort lines with 100 Franc bills, I crawled inside my skin. The energy in the atmosphere that I was sensing became prickly and sharp. As my friends got high, I did my best to fit in. But it was uncomfortable.

Although I'm a friendly, socially active person, I've often felt isolated because of my intense sensitivity to energy. Some of my happiest times are those I have spent alone because I haven't had to fight off or adapt to people's energy. Most of the time in my youth I attracted gorgeous womanizing men who were drug addicts. Looking back, I think I was drawn to this type of man because deep inside, I knew they were the most sensitive. Doing drugs was a way for them to shut down their feelings. Seeing people so out of control with their emotions made me feel better about my own inability to create balance in my own life. It made me feel normal. My thinking was messed up.

The relationships we attract into our lives are never an accident. If you review your past, you will find that in your relationships you were always making a choice, even if that was to participate in an abusive relationship. My belief is that even being born into an abusive family is a pre-destined choice, involving deep spiritual learning for the soul. The purpose of pain is to embody more love, acceptance, and compassion for others.

I stayed in my drama and pain as long as I did because I thought my life would become boring and meaningless if I stopped feeling intense highs and lows. Despite all the pain, I had some exquisitely high moments in which I thought, "Wow, I'm so lucky. My life is amazing." Then I'd crash and burn, as I couldn't maintain peak emotions. It got to the point where I finally accepted that something had to change. The highs and lows were taking a toll on my soul. I separated myself from the London party scene, thinking this would solve all my problems. I believed that practicing yoga and pursuing my spirituality would make me whole and peaceful. But basically I was jumping out of the frying pan into the fire. I finally had to face that the problems I had were inside me.

For years I danced around and skimmed over my true feelings. I thought if I opened the dam of emotions inside of me, I'd drown in pain. By not acknowledging my feelings, by putting on a brave face and pretending everything was okay, I increased the turbulence of my emotions until, one day, I felt so much chaos that I couldn't run away from myself anymore. When I looked at myself in the mirror, I perceived the woman looking back at me as ugly and unlovable. No amount of makeup or designer clothing could take away that bad feeling. I realized that carrying intense amounts of pain inside me was impeding any possibility of long-term happiness. This was a turning point.

Until then, I had felt that my circumstances happened to me. Now I made a decision to let go of what was holding me back consciously and unconsciously, and to stop playing the role of the victim. No more feeling sorry for myself. I decided to make my sensitivity to emotions work for me in a more positive way, and that's when my life improved a thousand-fold. I didn't have to take on other peoples' emotions. It didn't make me a cold heartless person when I detached myself from experiencing what they were feeling. I could be helpful and a healer without sacrificing my well-being.

If you're already very sensitive to energy, you will understand exactly what I'm speaking of. If you are someone who has a hard time feeling and you think you are numb to emotions, you're likely to discover that you are much more sensitive than you realize.

Being Sensitive

A sensitive is someone who has heightened sensitivity to energy in his or her environment. An empath is someone who absorbs people's energy, usually without being aware he or she is doing this. If you are a sensitive, it is most likely you are also an empath and that you are most definitely clairsentient. However, if you are struggling to integrate this sensitivity in your life, your skill of clairsentience will work against you until you learn how to run energy through you without absorbing it.

Have you ever walked into a hotel room and felt uncomfortable or edgy in the space? If you answered yes, the reason you felt that way is that you were picking up on the emotional energy that emanated from the people who were in the room before you. The discomfort you felt was the residue of their thoughts and actions.

People who don't understand they are clairsentient will often suffer tiredness and depression because they are like sponges, constantly absorbing energy. But they won't correlate the irritation they are feeling with what someone else is feeling, or recognize that it is not their own feeling. They may not realize that the headache they picked up was someone else's headache.

For clairsentience to work in your favor, it is necessary to create strong energetic boundaries, so that you do not unconsciously take on the energy, pain, fears, and problems of those around you. It took me years to understand why I felt severe nausea when I went into a cancer ward and why I experienced intense claustrophobia when traveling on the subway. I still feel uncomfortable walking through large groups of people at large live events, like concerts, and spending time in airports. I have to consciously shut down my energy to be able to handle the concentration of energy created at large gatherings.

Your energy is doing things you are unaware of all the time. It extends and contracts, vibrates fast, and can get dense, slow, or stuck, depending on how you react to the environment and to the people with whom you interact. Clearing and containing your energy is a key factor in feeling good and maintaining emotional and physical health.

You are flesh and bones, however from the perspective of your sixth sense, you are comprised of particles of light. When I scan people's energy clairsentiently, I always look at them from this perspective, as it helps me to see the true nature of their situation and highlights any blocks that are not easily visualized. I've had clients ask, "How can you do as good an intuitive reading on the phone instead of me sitting in front of you?" It's possible because I'm looking at them in the form of particles of light.

I also like doing phone readings because the distance between a client and me makes it easier for me to detach from the client's energy and supports greater objectivity. Because I'm empathetic and sensitive to energy, a client sitting in front of me can leave me feeling exhausted. In person, our energy fields are directly connected.

If you're a professional intuitive and very sensitive, doing sessions on the phone instead of in person with your clients will help you keep your energy levels high. The biggest problem I see psychics and energy healers go through is burnout, which is the result of running other people's energy through their own nervous systems. I show how to effectively run energy through you without absorbing it in the Intuition Development System™. Even if you're physically strong, your body needs to be respected and treated well to ensure a healthy long life.

One time I was working with a client at her home. Her problem was constant exhaustion. She wanted me to see what was causing it and have it cleared. I closed my eyes and tuned in, however I couldn't see anything. No guidance seemed to be presented. Then I felt a sharp pain go through my chest. It was as if a large amount of steel had been placed on me like a heavy suit of armor. "Are you okay?" my client asked. I'd turned ghostly white and felt awful. "I'm fine," I replied, gritting the pain into my teeth.

A scene suddenly flashed in my mind's eye clairvoyantly. My client had drowned on a boat with a group of people. I could feel the pain not only of her, but also of all the other people on that boat. I gave her a healing and extracted that energy. As I left her home, she said, "Wow, I feel great, it's as if a weight has been lifted from me."

It had. Now I was carrying it. I'd cleared her energy and trauma by running it through my body as if I were a garbage disposal. That experience put me in bed. My back was in so much agony that I could barely twist my torso. I decided that I would go to a chiropractor if it hadn't cleared up by the third day. Thankfully the pain lasted no more than two days. This was strong confirmation to me that even though we don't see energy, it is powerful, real, and can have a negative impact if we are not aware of it.

Everyone has the ability of clairsentience. The problem with this is that most of us live in environments that numb our sensitivity to energy and instead heighten irritation. Electrical equipment and noise pollution bombards and weakens our energy field on a daily basis. Then if we eventually do take a well-deserved vacation where it is peaceful and calm, like on the beach in Hawaii, we feel wired, unable to relax, and hypersensitive to everything. The good news is that there are techniques we can practice to alleviate the energy stresses that impact us.

As a culture, we have moved so far away from balance and harmony that an internal belief has been created in many people's minds that true peace, harmony, and happiness do not exist except for the few who are rich and famous. But wealth and fame in fact do not protect any of us from going through emotional turmoil.

The key to handling your sensitivity is to deepen your ability to feel energy without taking the weight of pain into yourself. You can be close to someone, support him or her, and be compassionate without having to carry his or her emotional and energetic burdens. If you are someone who often plays the roll of the martyr, taking on other people's problems, this is a strong indication that you are extremely sensitive to energy and likely have old wounds stored in your own body at a cellular level.

When you detach yourself from feeling other people's energy, your ego mind will think it will be cut off, rejected, and unloved. In reality, as you draw your energetic awareness back inside yourself and away from those around you two things happen. First, the person upon whom you have unknowingly been imposing your energy feels as if he or she can breathe again. This person will be more receptive to you. Second, you can spot your denial and pain because your awareness is now focused inwards.

You constantly live your life housing lifetimes of old wounds. We all do. These cannot be cleared from your body if you are not present to yourself. When you know what you are feeling, why you are feeling it, and where the feeling came from, this will give you the ability to quickly release the energy that is creating pain in your life. The reason you would hold on to old energy is that you're not sure what it is or why it's there. This is like keeping old clothes and objects you no longer use; you keep them just in case you might need them, when in truth you outgrew them a long time ago.

When you stop focusing outside of yourself and begin looking inside, a strong internal confidence develops that attracts the types of people you want to have in your life and leads you to being in an environment you want to be in. Miscommunications, resistance, and power struggles in relationships disappear. They are replaced with a greater sense of love, caring, and intimacy.

When you first open to this new way of being, it usually triggers feelings of awkwardness, emptiness, and abandonment. If your energy has been far out of alignment, when you bring it back to its natural state of being you could feel weird and out of synch. You may want to go back to how things were. Remind yourself that what you've been feeling up to this point hasn't worked well for you. If you truly want to have a new experience, you've got to practice a different way of being. The raw feelings you may have as you develop greater inner awareness will transform into peaceful reassurance. Learning how to trust your intuition will serve you well in every aspect of your life.

Feeling the Truth

Clairsentience allows you to feel the truth. It doesn't matter what a person says to you, your feelings will indicate what's really happening. When people don't understand why they feel how they feel, they go to a psychic for answers. But often, in the process, they are guided to take incorrect action steps. There's nothing more empowering and confidence boosting than getting your own insights and acting upon your wisdom. If everyone did this, people would stop blaming each other for failed relationships.

As you become aware, you will be able to feel other people's intentions and unintentional denial. This will help you be compassionate with them, because you will be able to sense that they're doing the best they can.

Your clairsentience will keep you in touch with your body's needs. It will help you know what foods are good for you and the types of exercise that would be beneficial. Your body is unique. Following someone else's techniques may not get you your desired results. As you begin to understand the subtleties of your body, you'll be able to prevent illness because you will be attuned to what is happening in your emotional body. Your body knows the truth of every situation beyond words, beyond the mind. Mindset tools are fantastic, however if you use such techniques to ignore your body and spirit you will reach only a fraction of your potential. Focusing on your needs and desires through the mind alone can take you only so far in your personal development.

You can kid yourself that you have everything you need because you're earning six or seven figures, however, without sensitivity, you are cutting yourself off from the possibility of feeling the resonance and depth of your soul. I was fortunate to grow up having all my financial needs met, so much so, that I didn't know what it was like to go without. My family treated me to several five-star luxury vacations each year, yet I often felt a huge, empty hole inside of me. Success is important for developing self-esteem, but let's not overlook self-love.

I listened to a success coach who I greatly respect a couple of weeks ago and she expressed her belief that intuition is "woo-woo," meaning nonsense. There have been many stories of when a mother has listened to her gut instinct and it has saved her child's life or an entrepreneur has rejected all the financial reports and gone on to take what seemed like a crazy risk, which was the turning point for his business. Those are examples of clairsentience. Sir Richard Branson and Bill Gates acknowledge intuition as a valuable contributing factor in their professional successes.

Ten years ago, I was brought on as a producer for a movie that had distribution in theaters across the U.K. Before we went into production, the director of the movie was excited about working with a certain lighting and camera company whose owner had been an executive on several movies for a big American studio. When we went to meet the owner, my stomach turned. Something felt off. "I don't like this deal. There's a piece of information that's being kept from you," I said to the director/ producer of the movie.

"What is it?" he said.

"I don't know, it's just a feeling I have," I said.

"Well unless you can prove it, we're going ahead with this company," he said.

I knew that if it didn't work with those companies, the movie wouldn't be made. On the quiet, I went and took meetings with another lighting and camera company and set the deals in place on standby. On the day that the original deal was to be signed I took the production manager aside who was working for the former American studio executive and I double bluffed her.

"I know something shady is going on with this deal, what is it?" I asked.

She looked shifty. "I don't know anything about the deal," she said.

"Come on, I won't say it was you," I said.

She paused then confessed, "He has $75,000 worth of debt from his last failed movie, so he's planning to use your production budget to pay off the debt. He doesn't even have the equipment he's promised you."

There was my proof. I went right to the director and got our allocated production manager to tell him. He was shocked, as it was four days before production was supposed to start. Thankfully, I already had the other deals lined up and ready to go for him.

Sometimes, you can't see proof, but your body can feel it. Think back now to a time when you used your intuition. Did you notice how your body spoke to you through feeling?

To help you understand what your body is trying to tell you, study the following list of some of the physical sensations you may experience and their meanings.

- Tingling means new awareness is coming to light. Unconscious thoughts are becoming conscious understanding. Tingling is most likely to occur while you are meditating or practicing yoga.

- Buzzing confirms that healing is taking place at a cellular level. Dense energy is being alchemized and raised to a higher frequency. Buzzing usually starts in one part of the body, like a foot, and will very quickly move up the leg, then travel through both legs, as well as the hands and arms. It feels amazing, like you're a light bulb radiating light for miles. When meditating, receiving Reiki, or any type of hands-on healing work, you may have this sensation.

186

- Pins and needles mean that blocked and stagnant energy is releasing. This feels uncomfortable, however it is a good sign. Pins and needles are usually followed by buzzing in the cells or by the development of extreme hot spots in the body (see below). This sensation is most likely to happen while meditating or practicing yoga.

- Hot spots and flushes represent new powerful energy flowing into your body and deep regenerative healing.

- Coldness in a warm environment is an indication that you need to ground yourself and get present in your body. You may be disconnected from your life purpose. It can also mean fear of getting hurt in relationship.

- Goose bumps are positive communication from a spirit guide or guardian angel that wants to make its presence known to you. It also means that your intuition is increasing.

- Shivers up and down the spine mean that an unseen energy or spirit is trying to communicate to you and make its presence known.

- A crawling sensation on the surface of your skin means that someone has invaded your energy boundaries. You need to address this sooner rather than later, so it doesn't quickly turn into a physical illness. This sensation could be accompanied by the symptom of nausea.

- Nausea has a few dominant meanings. First, it may mean that a situation you are in denial about needs to be resolved. Second, it may mean that you have weak boundaries around certain people. If so, you need to go inwards and ask who is invading my energy? Third, it may mean you are downloading new positive energy into your physical body faster than you are releasing old negative energy. If so, take time out to clear the old energies and integrate the new energy.

- Numbness means you have trauma or old pain trapped inside you. When you release it, there can be the feeling of floodgates opening, usually followed by tears that help soften your energy as the numbness disperses.

- Itchy skin suggests that you look inwards and be honest with yourself about who or what situation is irritating you in your life.

- A nervous twitch in your eye means your physical body is struggling to integrate all the new energy that is flowing into you. This is most likely to happen when you have been studying a lot of material and are in self-education mode. The twitch should last no more than two to three weeks. Practice meditation and yoga during this period to help balance your body if you have this symptom.

- A sharp, sudden pain in an isolated part of the body usually means that you are feeling the impact of a negative thought that has been directed towards you.

- Dull aching represents a situation in which you are procrastinating. It can also be a warning sign that the situation or relationship will worsen quickly if you do not take a decisive action soon.

- Tugging in solar plexus means you are handing your power away in a relationship. You are not trusting or respecting yourself. When you feel this sensation you need to pull your energy back into your own body and set a solid boundary, because the other person, usually a lover or boyfriend, is feeding off of your energy and is not flowing good energy back to you.

- Butterflies in your belly signal that you have made a connection with someone whose energy is elevating your vibration and consciousness. This is also an indication that you need to center your energy, ground yourself, and slow down. Let the energy settle before you rush into anything, like jumping into bed (I'm not talking about sleeping).

- A blanket of weight over the body that feels like lead spirals you into depression. The weight is the crash and burn from being in a high frequency and then falling back to where you were. It now feels bad being where you are because you've had a taste of more refined energy. Sparkling wine tastes fine until you've had champagne. You catch my drift?

- Headaches confirm that your mind is clogged with excess thoughts or you are on information overload. Each type of headache has a slight variation of meaning.

- Pain in the base of the skull can represent unexpressed feelings. It can also be intangible thoughts that are jumbled and have not yet come into conscious awareness. The pain at the base of the skull is letting you know they are about to come to the surface. Taking an analgesic will dampen your awareness and sensitivity, and slow down your soul's progress by impeding this opportunity for spiritual growth.

- A migraine in which you feel like your head is split down the middle or as if you have a plate of steel stuck in the center of your head, signals that you are conflicted about an important relationship or a life changing decision you need to make.

- A migraine in which you feel as if a band of pressure around the forehead, almost like a clamp, is slowly being tightened means that your clairvoyance is strengthening. The reason it hurts so much is that an energetic veil of protection, like a shell, has been around your head and the pain represents you breaking through that shell. It may sound strange, but pain can be a sign that you are making positive developments.

- The sensation of light feathers touching the surface of your skin confirms that your guardian angel or spirit guides are making their presence felt and also that they are in a playful mood. My spirit guides gently touch the top of my head, arm, or nose to get my attention.

- Palpitations or fluttering in your heart suggests deep spiritual expansion is occurring. You may have been doing a lot of spiritual reflection and healing of late that has increased your sensitivity to energy, as well as created an influx of energy into your physical body. I used to worry there was something wrong with my heart or that I was having a heart attack. But I found my palpitations never lasted more than a few days. Palpitations can also indicate stress. If you believe that to be the case, better to be on the safe side and schedule an appointment with your medical doctor immediately.

Boundary Setting Technique

Here's a boundary setting technique I use before going into a social setting. Begin by taking a couple of deep breaths into your body to draw your awareness inside yourself.

Then run through the following boundary checklist. By clarifying your own thoughts and physical feelings you can quickly recognize if you have taken on someone else's energy.

- How do you feel? Tired? Energized? Nervous? Happy?

- Do you have any pains or tension in your body? Headaches?

- What mood are you projecting for the environment you are about to step into?

- Do you feel positive or negative about the outcome?

- Do you feel grounded, distracted, scattered, or calm?

Next, visualize, sense, and feel yourself pulling your energy back inside of your physical body and sealing it in with an outline of gold light. Otherwise your energy could easily get scattered without you realizing it. Energy can be like clothes left lying out on a chair. Get into the habit of hanging them back up in the closet before you enter a new environment. This will ensure you conserve your energy.

Have you ever decided you're fed up with the way you're being treated by a lover, and just as you've let go and moved on psychologically, he text messages you or calls? That's because he felt you establish an energetic boundary with him. The guy may not be consciously aware of it, but boy did he feel it!

Benefits of Clairsentience

One of the main benefits of clairsentience is being able to feel your true emotions, including those that would that sabotage you and lie beneath consciousness. Being able to sense the riptides in energy that often pull you in a direction you don't want to go means you will have confidence to make right choices. Awareness will stop overwhelm and fear.

Clairsentience can save you from a lot of heartache by ensuring that you don't invest your time in loveless relationships. The writing is always on the wall from day one. When you are aware of the physical sensations in your body and tune-in to your emotions, you will be able to trust your spontaneity and avoid impulsiveness.

I have seen many mixed up women who feel scared to go with the flow and follow their hearts when they meet an awesome guy, but who are willing to hand their vulnerable heart over on a silver platter to a dubious guy who has no qualms about breaking it with a sledgehammer. They aren't yet attuned to their feelings. I'll say the same thing to you that I've told them. Listen to your body, feel your emotions, and you'll be led to experience love and intimacy beyond your expectations. Mr. Right could be standing in front of you and yet because of past wounding being triggered unconsciously inside of your body, you dismiss him. Open your heart to feeling. When you do this, emotions can run effortlessly through you. When emotions are stopped this causes pain. Breathe and feel. This is not rocket science. Feelings are meant to be felt.

Here are some emotions you may experience when it comes to affairs of the heart:

Love, pain, fear, jealously, anxiety, happiness, openness, receptivity, frustration, anger, resentment, low self-esteem, ecstasy, joy, generosity, vulnerability, playfulness, intensity, pressure, lightness, desire, repulsion, disgust, distrust, hate, serenity, acceptance, understanding, judgment, neediness, irritation, kindness, warmth, passion, and lust.

There is a spectrum of emotional energy you may feel in your heart. Sometimes you'll feel several emotions simultaneously. You can love and hate someone, and be attracted to someone and repulsed by him, too. Emotions are not black and white. They are multicolored. The most important step you can take is to begin observing your emotions. Just watch and feel. This will help you be a clear channel for greater understanding, peace, and love to be experienced in your daily life.

In my early thirties, I took everything so bloody personally. I knew the concept of feeling my feelings, but I hadn't felt them freely yet. I kept a part of myself closed. That part of me was scared of being judged by my friends. I had to remind myself that if they judged me, they really were not friends. I was a wounded bird who shied at everything. I thought I was strong and happy-go-lucky, but all the while I was pouring my attention into trying to make emotionally unavailable men love me. Every time I got rejected, it was like a knife had been stuck in my heart. My ego mind skillfully chose to create those situations. My unconscious mind was leading me directly into pain.

For a while, I thought guys were idiots, however I felt satisfaction when a nice guy liked me and I could reject him. How messed up is that? And the pain from the relationships I knew I shouldn't be in only worsened. I felt like a love junkie who was numb inside, whose heart had turned to stone.

When I finally let a reliable, trustworthy man into my heart (my husband Nick), my heart fluttered and I panicked. My ego mind promptly said, "You're hopeless at this love thing and he doesn't really want you." So I nearly screwed up and relapsed into my old pattern of rejecting a special man. Thank goodness, my soul was stronger than my ego. I said, "Ego, thanks very much for your opinion, now bugger off."

All it actually took was making a decision. The fear I'd felt inside my body was not a warning that entering into a relationship with Nick would end disastrously. It was my old unprocessed pain coming into my consciousness. As soon as I was aware, I was able to process and release the pain, at which point I felt liberated to love. As you get more adept at recognizing your emotions and understanding the signs your body is giving you, you'll be able to clearly see the difference between good guidance and a fear-based action, too. You'll be able to override your ego mind and follow your intuition.

Trusting your clairsentience and knowing its language will enable you to live your life purpose. You won't waste time in a job that bores you. Instead you'll have enough courage to leave. You'll feel creativity inside you that you weren't aware of. Even when there are no external signs that you made the right decision to stop climbing the corporate ladder and become an entrepreneur, you'll be able to feel the rightness of your choice inside. Your clairsentience will help you through emotionally turbulent times, as you transition from one industry to another. It will nurture your personal development. You'll never need to see a career counselor again regarding what industry to choose to work in, as you'll just follow your intuition.

You know what's best for you. Stop looking at what others are doing around you. Don't limit yourself because you think you have to have certain resources to be a success. Billionaires like Bill Gates and The Google boys began their businesses out of their garages. Instead of wasting your energy on excuses, start feeling what you'd love to be doing on a daily basis and then take a first step to make it happen. Go read an autobiography of someone who has done something similar to what you want to do, and model that person's actions with your own unique character and personality.

Clairsentience can highlight the cause of financial blocks in your life. Once you become aware of your underlying emotions, you will be able to see how you are stopping your money flow. If you have been passive in approaching your goals and you are not making precise choices, be aware that you can only create mediocre results. Feel what you truly want in every cell of your body, heart, and soul and go after it.

One of my clients is smart, beautiful, and brilliant, however she had a core feeling of being undeserving that was repelling new business prospects. She couldn't understand how this was happening. As we looked closely at her energetic patterns, it was apparent that her soul was getting kicked out of her body by her ego every time she was about to receive financial abundance. Thus she had sabotaged her success. The way she broke through this challenge was to hold firm when fear arose in her body and do the opposite of what her fear told her. When she procrastinated, she would force herself to take action. Within a few months of doing this, my client's higher self had a stronger presence in her body than her ego mind. She not only cleared her old blocks, she also created a new energy that supported her in creating effortless results and reaching her financial goals.

You can develop strong clairsentience in a matter of weeks if you consistently practice awareness of your body and emotions. You will begin to see a direct correlation between how your mind affects your emotions and your physical wellbeing. It will become clear what situation or person has triggered a feeling within you. You'll be able to quickly recognize when you have absorbed someone else's beliefs and emotions, and you will be able to counter this with grounding or centering meditation. Awareness alone can get you into alignment with the wise part of your soul.

Be gentle with yourself as you develop your clairsentience. If you've ignored your wounds for a long time, when you open to your feelings from the perspective of the sixth sense a pitfall to be aware of is feeling vulnerable and unattractive. It is best to process strong emotions alone or with a confidante you can trust, but not with a person who has triggered you. Otherwise you could find yourself saying things you regret that later on will make you cringe. When I look back at some of my conversations with ex-boyfriends I feel awful. I was over-reactive and blaming. Instead I should have removed myself from the situations in which my needs weren't being met.

If you're going through a separation or have recently divorced, be extra-attentive to your feelings. You are more sensitive than you realize. Only when you look back will you have heightened clarity about your situation. When you understand that emotions are like weather, one minute stormy and the next a clear blue sky, you'll find it easier to be present to what is happening in your life now. Unprocessed emotions pull you into your past by default, instead of by choice. Master your clairsentience and you will enjoy the range of emotions and feelings you have in a whole new way.

The purpose of your clairsentience is to keep you on track in your life. It is a navigational tool to help guide you to the best outcome in love, work, and play. Your clairsentience can ward off illness and problems before they manifest in your life. I like to look at it as preventive medicine.

If you're someone who is already incredibly sensitive and you feel your clairsentience is overwhelming I recommend that you focus on drawing your energy inwards and stop trying to feel the energy of those around you. You may think you're blocking people's energy and wonder why you feel even worse. When you try and shut the energy out, you put up a wall of resistance to yourself that absorbs external energy even faster. The most effective emotional state to practice is being neutral. This will ensure you do not attract or repel energy. So take five minutes a day to sit quietly with your feet firmly on the ground and breathe. Feel the magnetic energy of the Earth drawing up through the soles of your feet and into your body where it can neutralize emotional electrical charges.

A good first step is to make notes daily in your intuition journal of all the physical sensations and emotions that you experience. This will help you unearth any unconscious patterns that are holding you back from realizing all your heart's desire.

As a beginner you may feel like nothing is happening or you will have dramatic sensitivity. Which occurs depends on how naturally sensitive you are and how much past wounding you carry at a cellular level. You will eventually find that your clairsentience is like being on a rollercoaster. After you go on the ride several times you will be able to anticipate the dips, drops, and loops of your energy. Then the ride will be exhilarating instead of frightening. You will come to understand you are safe when you stay on track.

Your biggest challenge may be an addiction to thrill seeking and the deep feelings of highs and lows. If you practice staying on track, you'll find that the highs and lows transform into expansiveness. This feeling of awareness will enable you to gain new ideas and insights you would not ordinarily notice. This is the sixth sense at its best.

Chapter 9

TUNE IN. TRUST IT:
Practicing Claircognizance

"I rely far more on gut instinct than researching huge amounts of statistics." —Sir Richard Branson

The way I tune into my intuition and trust it is by getting quiet enough to know that when I find an answer—when it emerges— I know beyond a shadow of a doubt that it is true. My intuition has not failed me. However I learned the hard way. I'd have an intuition, think to myself, "That's stupid," ignore the guidance, and then kick myself later because my gut instinct had been dead on. After many mistakes, I decided to practice following my intuition no matter what. Because when I didn't, I never got what I wanted. Usually this guidance related to boys. Yes, I attracted boys, but ones who didn't treat me how I wanted to be treated. I grew up reading fairytales like "Cinderella" and "Snow White" and I knew inside that one day my prince would come. Thank goodness he did eventually show up and he is ridiculously romantic. On the year anniversary of Nick's proposal to me, he took me to the Ritz Carlton in Marina del Rey, California, for dinner. We were sipping pink champagne and Nick began chuckling a little. "What's so funny?" I said.

"Great champagne," he said, pausing on the word champagne.

"Yes it is," I said, still oblivious to his surprise. You'd think because I'm psychic I would have realized there was a pink pearl necklace in the bottom of the champagne flute, but I didn't. Nick finally had to ask, "What's in your glass?" Then I peered inside and saw the necklace resting peacefully beneath the bubbles. Nick carefully put the necklace around my neck, admired it, and kissed me. It was a dream come true to be wrapped in love.

When Nick proposed to me after six months of dating, some of my friends said, "Wow, that's quick. How do you know he's 'The One'?"

"Because I know," I said.

"How do you know?" one of my friend's asked again.

"It's a resounding *yes* from deep inside of me," I said.

In the realm of the sixth sense, this skill is called *claircognizance*. You just know the answer. You don't have to think about it, feel it, see it, or hear it, because you just know it. The more you trust what you know, the stronger this ability gets.

I love the feeling of clarity that claircognizance gives me. You could rationalize it as purely life experience, however I know it's more than that. Especially, when it is knowing things you couldn't possibly know. I remember when my Grandma Rita, that's my mom's mom had cancer. I was 20. Grandma was in a nursing home located a five-minute walk from our cute mews house in Hampstead, London. On a summer Friday evening, Mom, Auntie Jill (Mom's sister), and my cousins Laura, Robert, John, and I congregated with a doctor and Grandpa Walter, who had been married to Rita for over sixty years. They were an amazing couple, who always brought our family together for delicious Friday night dinners and endowed us with our strong family values.

The doctor talked of a new medication to ease Grandma Rita's pain.

"What's the point?" I asked. "She's about to die."

"No she's not," Mom said.

I felt awful for Mom, as she was so close with Grandma, but I hadn't yet developed enough awareness to keep my mouth shut when I knew something painful.

"She's going to die any day now. I know it," I said.

"I don't want to hear any more of this talk," Mom said.

If you have strong claircognizance and it's a situation you cannot change, be sensitive to others' emotions. Just because you feel bad doesn't mean you have to make someone else feel bad also.

The next afternoon I had planned to go to a nightclub called L'Equipe Anglaise with a couple of friends. As a London party girl, I knew I had to pace myself, so I would often take afternoon naps before hitting the dance floor 'til the early hours of the morning. That afternoon, I lay down on my bed at 4 P.M. and set my alarm for 7 P.M. As I closed my eyes I had the strongest knowing I've ever had in my life. "Grandma is dying."

I sat bolt upright and quickly grabbed a pair of denim shorts and a tee shirt. I tied my hair in braids and found Mom sitting downstairs alone watching TV. "Mom, I'm going to see Grandma. I think she's dying," I said.

"No darling, she's doing well. I saw just left her a couple of hours ago."

"I need to go see her," I said.

"Of course, if you want to go . . . " Mom said.

"I do," I said. With urgency in my step, I walked quickly over the cobbled stones on my street, hoping my intuition was wrong.

As I entered the nursing home, I could smell death. It hung in the air and made me feel slightly queasy. I took the elevator up to my Grandma's ward and found the nurse who was on duty. "How is Rita Harris?" I asked.

"She's doing well on the new medication her doctor prescribed her," the nurse said.

"Can I go see her?" I said.

"Of course," the nurse said.

Several other beds filled with cancer victims shared the same space with Grandma Rita. I walked around to Grandma Rita's left side, pulled up a plastic chair by the side of her bed, and took her left hand in mine. I could see that her breathing was shallow. I thought back to a conversation Grandma Rita and I had the day before. "I'm done Joanna. I don't want to live anymore," Grandma Rita had told me.

"Don't say that Grandma," I said.

"I'm tired. I'm so tired," Grandma Rita said.

I chocked back tears. One escaped down my cheek.

Here I was the following day, sitting beside Grandma again. She was unconscious, but I knew she could hear me, I just knew it. As I held her hand, I began to feel intense nausea and lightheadedness. I could feel the life force, Grandma's spirit, moving out of her body fast. "Don't go Grandma, I'll be right back. I need to get Mom and Auntie Jill so they can say goodbye to you," I said.

A woman in the opposite bed from Grandma gave me a sympathetic look. I knew she had seen death before. I ran down the corridor to the nurse's station. "I think my Grandma's dying, can you come look?" I said.

"Yes, dear," the nurse said, trying to keep up with me as I walked quickly back to Grandma's bed.

The nurse took her pulse and said, "Yes, she's going to pass any moment."

"Please can you call my Mom and Aunt?" I said.

"Yes dear, you stay here with your Grandma."

I took Grandma Rita's hand again and the nausea quickly returned. I leaned in close and said, "Mom and Auntie Jill are on their way. Please wait for them to say goodbye."

The ten minutes I sat with Grandma felt like an eternity, it took me all my will to stay connected with Grandma as I felt each ounce of life force leave her body. A minute after Mom and Auntie Jill had arrived by Grandma's bed, she passed to the other side. How did I know that would happen? I just knew.

My Grandpa Walter feared death. I was also with him as his spirit left his body, however because his fear was so intense medication kept him alive for a few months afterwards. He was physically alive, but he wasn't there in his body. I'd already seen and felt his spirit lift out of his body. I knew he was gone.

When my Grandpa Lou Lou, that's my dad's dad, was very ill, I happened to be staying close to the hospital he was staying in. We hadn't spoken for some time because of my foolishness with my ex-fiancé. I remember standing in the kitchen and again having a distinct knowing, "Grandpa is going to die." I felt so stupid going to the hospital, especially because I know Grandpa didn't want to see me. When I arrived in his room the first thing he said was, "Go away Joanna. I don't want to see you."

That hurt so much. I'd thrown away years of love because of my arrogance regarding spirituality. Grandpa had given me many privileges that he'd had to work so hard for. He originally came to England from Poland with six siblings, including a twin brother. His family was very poor and he went on to become a self-made millionaire. Grandpa Lou Lou used to puff on his cigar with a glass of whiskey and a small dish of nuts and say, "PMA, what does it mean Joanna?"

"Positive mental attitude," I said.

"That's right. I learned that from Napoleon Hill and that's how I became successful," he said, as we sat in his beautiful house in St. Johns Wood, London.

Now, here he was in a small private room of a hospital up the street, and I stood before him in a failed relationship, stone cold broke financially. "I know you don't want to see me Grandpa. I just came by to say I'm sorry and I love you."

"Come here," Grandpa said.

I walked cautiously towards him and he extended his hand. I took it. "I'm so disappointed in you Joanna. I didn't expect you to behave like you have," he said.

Tears welled up in my eyes. "I know I've let you down and I'm so sorry," I said.

"It's hard dying. My body's failing, yet my mind is sharp," Grandpa said.

I nodded.

"I'm scared," Grandpa said.

"I know. That's why I'm here for you," I said.

"Do you think there's anything more once you die?" he said.

"I know there is Grandpa. I just know it," I said.

"I love you, Joanna," Grandpa said.

I knew that would be the last time I would see him. Grandpa died several hours later. I had given up on myself and yet my intuition guided me to higher understanding. Grandpa Lou Lou always quoted Winston Churchill, *"Never, never, never never give up."*

The day Grandpa died, my persistence was ignited once more. There was purpose to my life although I had deviated and sidestepped on my path. I knew it was now time to get back on track and start using my intuition. It never had gone away. I'd abandoned it.

My good news is that my Grandma Darling, Dad's mom, is alive and well. I call her every week in London. We have an excellent relationship.

The way I know I'm right about something is that I feel a sense of determination and bull-headedness. Someone may kindly make a suggestion to me and I will know that it's not relevant to me. Or someone suggests a class or a referral and I just know it's not for me. I'm quite particular in that I don't like people making recommendations if I don't ask for them, especially when someone says, "You should go and see this really great psychic . . ." That's when I smile sweetly through gritted teeth (yes, I'm human) and say, "Thank you for your suggestion."

I used to spend hours on the phone asking friends what I should do about a guy I liked or discussing the meaning of my life and what I was supposed to be doing. I don't need to do that anymore. Now when I meet someone, I can feel that person's energy and I know whether I want to get to know the person better, be friends, and spend time together. If someone says that he or she had the most wonderful work experience with a particular company and I'm not feeling it for myself, I don't hesitate to say, "No thank you." A big aspect of claircognizance is being able to trust your no. It's often harder saying no than saying yes. Many people get themselves in a right old mess because they say yes for fear of missing an opportunity or failing to make a decision.

When you develop clarity about what is meant to be in your life, you'll save hours and hours of time. Instead of talking it over on the phone or worrying about a situation, you can be out in the world creating your dream life and having quality good times with family and friends. Your health automatically improves because you don't fear your choices. You know your choices are right for you.

Remember, every person's life is unique. The more attuned you are to your needs, the greater your understanding of how to fulfill your desires will be. Often when I work with my clients and ask what their goals are, they look at me sheepishly and say, "I don't have any goals. I don't know what I want." No wonder they've been stuck.

If you let life happen to you, nothing is going to happen. In your heart you know what you want. The reason you unconsciously fear what you want is that you imagine it's too big or you'll never get it. Well, either way, with this approach you're not getting it.

When you step on to the path of claircognizance, peace and knowing permeate every aspect of your life. Even when you are faced with challenges, you will find that you are able to stay calm and centered. Low self-esteem dissolves. I've stood in front of the mirror so many times in the past and felt hideous. I'd walk into a party and feel like people were thinking, "She's ugly and pathetic," when they looked at me. That's because I thought they knew more than me. I thought they knew better. It took me a long time to learn that what other people think isn't relevant to my life. Whether someone likes me, thinks I'm funny or finds me attractive doesn't determine my beauty, wisdom or strength.

As I accepted the gift of claircognizance, I noticed the wall of protection I'd held up for so long finally coming down. I realized it took me a lot of effort to keep people at a distance and I didn't like the cold edge that I could feel emanating from me towards them. When I see other people give off aloof energy, I know they are wounded and insecure. So the expression, "Don't take it personally," is good advice. It truly isn't aloofness against you if you know in your heart that you've been the best, kindest, most compassionate person possible.

If you're new to using claircognizance, you'll find that you have days that you're totally in the zone. Other times you're going to fall prey to fear and insecurity. This is just part of the developmental process. It took me years to understand that I was experiencing claircognizance. There were many circumstances in which I would have created a more beneficial outcome if I had known to trust my gut. Of all the sixth sense skills, claircognizance is the most rewarding because it awakens absolute knowing and peace inside you. Remind yourself that there's no pressure or rush to accomplish claircognizance. Enjoy the learning curve. It's well worth it.

I encourage you to practice this skill with only simple choices initially. I do not recommend using your claircognizance to buy a home, end a marriage, or change careers until you have been practicing this skill for several years and you know that your intuition is correct. When I have a big decision to make, my claircognizance presents me with an action step. Then I check in with my clairvoyance, clairaudience, and clairsentience for confirmation, and I give myself thirty days to decide. Be aware that it is easy to get caught up in the panic of having to make an immediate decision. That's not a good idea, especially if it's a costly one that will take years to resolve.

There's a time for spontaneity, but make sure that's appropriate for you first. As soon as I feel I need to rush into something because I fear losing an opportunity, I let go and step back. I get clear about my goal and put a plan in place, and then I move forward.

Claircognizance will eliminate blaming others for your choices. It will also help you think more deeply about your actions before you take them. Sometimes you will recognize mistakes that friends and family members are making. But if they don't ask for your advice, don't give it. Instead be loving and supportive to them. This doesn't mean endorse poor behavior or lend money (it's unlikely you'll get it back), rather do your best to love them from a perception of detachment. People will appreciate your goodness. They'll always be happy to see you and enjoy being in your presence.

Everyone has the skill of claircognizance. The environment that you grew up in and the way you were taught at school will affect how attuned you are to it. A first step you can take to begin awakening claircognizance in your life is to feel the answer from deep inside of you. I've found that when I've been out of tune with myself, it feels like I have a bottomless black pit in my stomach. When I'm in tune, it feels like there's a powerful magnet inside me that emanates good energy. The more I focus on it, the stronger it gets, and the more I trust the guidance I receive.

If you've never consciously practiced using the skill of claircognizance before, give yourself three months before you anticipate seeing results. You may have success before then, but it takes consistent focus and awareness to integrate this skill into your life. This is a lifestyle change. Eventually you won't have to think about activating your claircognizance, it will become a natural occurrence that touches everything you do.

Chapter 10

GIVE YOURSELF PERMISSION

"Follow your instincts. That's where true wisdom manifests itself."
—*Oprah Winfrey*

The block to developing your intuition is not giving yourself permission to trust the intuitive guidance you receive from your six senses. You now have increased awareness about intuition. Will you allow yourself to perceive it?

The Psychic Pathway

I immersed myself in the world of the sixth sense because I need to experience life deeply. Because I'm a Scorpio mediocre doesn't work for me. I live for love, passion, and happiness. I was driven to develop my intuition because the joy of celebrating my clients' successes far outweighed any personal pain I experienced in the process. Eventually, the scales tipped in my favor and the pain disappeared.

My pain left me because I kept facing it. When I was blocked, I looked even deeper inside to the parts of my soul that carried deep shame, remorse, and regret. By using my clairvoyance, I could find this pain more easily and unearth it quickly. What I've come to learn is that despite the intense feelings and pain that arise, the peace, love, and aliveness that occurs is so much greater. That's what drives me.

You Can Learn From My Mistakes

The biggest mistake I ever made was the mistake of not believing in myself. I thought someone else had to give me the love and success I wanted. I looked for that love in emotionally unavailable people and wondered why I felt so desperate, humiliated, and alone. I kept waiting for someone to discover my talents and felt resentful of successful people. Some convoluted part of my thinking justified that it was their responsibility to make me a success. I used to attract clients who expected me to wave a magic wand, like the Fairy Godmother in "Cinderella," and make their lives perfect because I was still carrying residues of this outward-looking energy in my unconscious mind. Like my clients, I was so busy complaining inside about what wasn't working in my life, and feeling overwhelmed and stuck at the prospect of reaching clarity, that I couldn't trust my intuition for my own life. This made me want to throw my intuition towel in every time.

This is why I had a love-hate relationship with being psychic for many years. When I could use my intuition to help a guy I wanted to date, I was irresponsible. Helping him was the way I justified my ulterior motives. At the time, I didn't realize I had an agenda. I couldn't understand why I felt so hurt and used after the guy got what he wanted. I can't blame any of those men. It wasn't their fault. I was using the power of my intuition to gain love and acceptance. It backfired on me because there are always karmic repercussions when you use the sixth sense for selfish personal gratification. Karma is the law of cause and effect. What you put out comes back to you. You can lie to yourself all you like, however you'll never find the peace and love your soul craves when you're true intention is not aligned with the actions you are taking.

When I look back on my relationship with my former fiancé, it is clear to me I could have left the relationship at any time. I created my own prison. I tried to control the way he loved me and manufacture the relationship. If I'd listened to my intuition, I never would have entered into a relationship with him, as his values and life goals were not aligned with mine. I tricked my own mind into believing I loved him because he wanted me and thought I was great. Or did he? It was my ego that stepped into that relationship. For it to work, I had to leave all my beauty, strength, and power at the door. My soul was left behind. As each day I committed more to the relationship, another part of my soul was put to sleep or fragmented. And, as more time passed, my life reflected these internal changes. It was a right old mess.

The only way I could heal from this pattern was to clear up my own crap. It would have been poor taste to let someone else clean up after me. My mom had been doing that a lot. She didn't have to, however she has a generous heart. Growing up, I took advantage of her giving nature. I didn't mean to. I know my parent's divorce affected me more than I realized. My motivations were led by fear of abandonment.

If you are stuck in any area of your life, whether it is in your finances, relationship, career, or health, it's not a coincidence. If you allow yourself to see, hear, feel, and know the truth, you'll be presented with a solution to the problem. The only reason that may be hard to believe is that you haven't sought clear guidance yet. Truly, you haven't because when you have, you'll know the solution.

I've discovered the path of least resistance in developing intuition is to acknowledge and accept yourself when you find a big, ugly albatross of negative energy trapped inside you. Don't scold, ignore, or maim it. That's futile. Nonetheless, it's often what people do. But realize that the more you try and hide it the more exhausting your life will get. It will take you away from focusing on your dreams and goals.

The psychic pathway, at its best, is magical and rewarding. The best thing that's happened to me since I've developed my intuition is that I like myself now. I had been oblivious for most of my life to how critical my ego mind was. If it wasn't criticizing me, it was negative about someone else. I discovered the key to transforming my ego into my best friend was to put it on stage in the spotlight. Knowing someone was paying attention always stumped it. Whereas backstage it could have done what it liked and gotten away with it.

Each one of your intuitive skills will allow you to remove pain effectively. Healers, therapists, psychics, and coaches can support your psychic transformation, however without you doing the work for yourself you'll never be entirely satisfied. That heaviness, a nagging feeling that you can't quite pinpoint but can sense is present, will not go away until you dig in deeply. I recommend you start listening to your mind, body, and spirit, because after you get over the initial shock about what you truly want and all your denial, you'll begin to feel amazing and craziness will be replaced with harmony.

I also encourage you to be vulnerable with people in your life who you know you can trust. If you go and pour your heart out to an old jealous school friend, a guy you've just started dating, or a parent who thinks you live on Mars since you got into "this intuition stuff," it's going to hurt you a lot. You'll feel like a leper and want to crawl under a stone and die. Also be aware of nosy fair-weather friends, co-workers, and acquaintances that ask you a lot of questions about your private life. These people make you feel you're living through the Spanish Inquisition. They seem concerned, but really they're digging around for your failures and dirt because they're not ready to look at their own unresolved issues. How will you recognize those people? Oh, believe me, you'll know as you start using your intuition on a consistent basis. You'll get a dropping feeling in your stomach and feel your aura shrink around you, that's how you'll know. And then you'll be able to hear your ego mind give you a good tongue-lashing. It hurts bad. The good news is that you'll be aware enough to avoid putting yourself in that predicament again. You'll be able to deflect their questions like brushing away an irritating fly.

Truly supportive people are excellent listeners. They allow you to express yourself. They understand that you have the answers you need inside of you. They're willing to be your audience and applaud your courage to step out on stage and take a risk.

Keep peeling back the layers of who you think you are each day and you'll meet your higher self. She'll be there for you in all her magnificence, full of wisdom. She'll extend her arms and wrap you in them. As you hold her, you'll feel her soft wings on her back, you'll know she's an angel. As you feel her power and strength, her unwavering conviction to emanate love at all times, all the pain of your past will dissolve. And when life gets tough and you have a challenging day, because sometimes you

215

will, it'll be easier to get through because you will know you are safe, protected, and loved.

The greatest lesson I've learned so far about my intuition is that I'm not alone. In the past, I cried myself to sleep in a ball and felt so very alone, abandoned, and unloved. I understand that the part of me who was crying was the separated part of my soul. I found that as I retraced my tracks and picked up the pieces of my broken heart and fragmented weathered soul, I felt a little more whole. I dusted them off and said, "I'm sorry I abandoned you. I was ashamed and embarrassed, will you forgive me?" Every time my soul forgave me.

Before I began writing this book, my friend Kim Castle urged me to be honest with people about who I am so they could clearly see that I'm not the psychic sitting at the right hand of God dispensing wisdom. It took me so long to get around to writing this book because I was paralyzed by the fear of what people would think of me. Well you're reading this now, so you know my dark secrets. I'm just a girl who grew up in North West London. There's nothing unordinary or special about me. I've had my ups and downs, my successes and failures. I don't have all your answers for you, but I know you can learn and apply to your own life what I've discovered as I traveled along my path of fascination with the world of the sixth sense. So the next time you're tempted to hand your bucks over to a neon street psychic who tells you that for $900 they can remove a curse from your life, my suggestion is tell them very nicely to get stuffed.

You Have a Unique Purpose

Believe me, you're definitely more psychic than those neon sign psychics and you're life isn't as bad as half of those phone psychics you can find online. The point I'm making is you have all the wisdom you need inside of you. Don't despair if you've been trying to use your intuition for a while and you've read lots of self-help books and you're still spinning in head boggling circles. When I was 11, I was brilliant at math. I scored between 97-100 percent on every exam I took because I could relate to my teacher Mrs. Glover. She was kind but tough. She challenged my answers and she encouraged me to push myself to go outside of my comfort zone. I also loved that she brought her little Jack Russell dog Tinker to class. At 14 my math results declined dramatically. I was consistently getting Cs and one day I failed. I couldn't believe it.

I knew I was great at math, so why wasn't I getting the results reflected? The teacher had changed. My math teacher at 14, Mrs. X, was impatient, critical, and skimmed over the surface. When I asked a question she got irritated. She looked at me as if I was stupid. She ridiculed me. As time progressed, I felt stupid. I felt ridiculous. I stopped asking questions and my grades declined. I thought I was a poor student even though it wasn't true. I'd had years of consistently good results before that. The failure was a breakdown in communication. There was a missing link in my being able to access the answers I needed.

There is no right or wrong style of intuitive communication. The only thing that matters is discovering how best you personally can access your intuition. Some people respond better to visual imagery, others to sound. Focus on the skill that interests you most. The way I became an excellent clairvoyant was that I was passionate about it. As a kid, I'd always been into art and painting, clairvoyance is a natural modality for me.

Don't try to be psychic. It's just a label to define use of the sixth sense. Relax into your intuition. Getting stressed about not being able to get results will stop you from seeing or feeling anything, and you'll only confuse yourself and get negative. You can do it. This isn't a super hero power. It's intuition and it is accessible to you right now, so give yourself permission to start exercising that muscle. Permission is the first step.

The thought of developing your intuition may seem a little daunting and scary at times, especially if you work in corporate America. However, you'll discover that you've already been using your intuition, albeit unknowingly. It's scary if suddenly you become aware that you shouldn't be blaming other people for what's happening in your life. You're responsible for your actions, emotions, and attitude. Your fear is getting it wrong. Everyone makes mistakes as they learn new skills. The key is to start with small tasks and graduate to bigger ones as you get more confident and adept in your practice. Start paddling in the shallow end before you dive into the deep end of the pool. Little steps and before you know it, you'll be a pro when it comes to trusting your own intuition.

You're going to feel so great when you start using your intuition. It's like getting membership to the Executive Club lounge at the airport and then being upgraded to the First Class lounge, which is full of perks and amenities you don't readily have access to. People who have never had access to either lounge will be none the wiser, however once you've tasted the lounge you're not going to want to go back to how things were before. Being psychic is not a privilege limited to a few lucky people. It's accessible to you now. Claim your membership to the club. You have a right to use your intuition. The only reason you may be holding yourself back is because you've been conditioned to believe that you don't deserve to, or that you have to be better, smarter, and more successful.

Open your eyes now. Stop walking around like a blind sheep following another sheep that doesn't know if it's going in the right or wrong direction. Regardless of where the sheep in front is going, the question to ask is, "What direction do I need to go in?" Your purpose is different from that other sheep's. You have a unique purpose. Ask yourself, "What is my life purpose?" The answer will come. You may hear it loud and clear right now or you may hear it a year from now. Whatever you do, don't give up on your intuition, as it won't let you down.

If you hear a little voice in your head say, "I'm stuck," reply to that part of yourself, "You're *not* stuck, you only think you are." All your barriers are self-imposed. This may be hard to believe if you've kept yourself trapped for a long time. I suggest that, as a first step, you commit to being receptive to your intuition. This action will gently open your sixth sense. You don't have to go through the rollercoaster I went through, in fact I recommend that you don't do it how I did it.

You are part of nature's cycle. Don't resist nature. Just be aware that there are times when you'll advance very quickly in the development of your intuition and other times it will feel like nothing is happening. In reality, the inner work is where the biggest transformation is occurring. Be patient because it *will* externalize itself in your life. Your body needs time to integrate energy. This is natural. Be gentle with yourself.

The greatest gift I received from incorporating intuition into my daily life is self-acceptance. It removed all the artificial pressures from every choice I needed to make. It had reached the point where I could see clearly whether it was best for one of my clients to stay in a relationship or leave, meanwhile I'd stand for 30 minutes in the supermarket weighing the decision of whether to have lamb or beef for dinner. Then, once I'd narrowed my choice down to steak, agonizing over what size piece of meat to buy.

You'll find that as you give yourself permission to have what you really want, you won't waste time procrastinating over what you think you deserve because you'll be totally attuned to the choices you are making and confident. Still think you don't know what you want? You do. Keep peeling back the layers.

My spirit guides just gave me a really cool clairvoyant image that they want me to relay to you. It's the image of one of those Russian nesting dolls that you open to find another smaller doll inside, and another inside that, and another, until finally you get to a whole doll which is solid and has substance, just like you.

Remind yourself daily, "I'm whole and perfect. I trust my intuition."

TEN ACTION STEPS TO UNLEASH THE PSYCHIC IN YOU

I urge you to remember that intuition is a muscle, which needs to be used daily to reap the benefits of trustworthy inner guidance and absolute clarity. If you commit to your intuition development, you'll get results that will amaze you!

Here are ten easy steps you can take to develop your intuition today.

- *Step #1* Sign up for my weekly online newsletter Confessions of a Psychic for FREE (valued at $197) at www.AmericasIntuitionCoach.com/ezine/joinus.

- *Step #2* Begin an intuition journal to record the aha's that you experience on your journey. To download your FREE Intuition Journal Pages visit: www.AmericasIntuitionCoach.com/journal.

- *Step #3* Get a rose quartz crystal, specifically for your intuition development. You can visit www.AuraShop.com for wonderful crystals.

- *Step #4* Ask your friends if they would like to share the journey of intuition development with you, be a support for each other, and connect with other like-minded people at www.IntuitionDevelopmentCircle.com.

- *Step #5* Do a daily meditation for five minutes a day. To download a FREE guided meditation visit www.AmericasIntuitionCoach.com/meditation.

- *Step #6* Find a yoga class in your area. Visit www.YogaWorks.com.

- *Step #7* Get outdoors and connect to the elements.

- *Step #8* Take time to relax, dream, and clear your head of excess thoughts.

- *Step #9* Create time to have fun and spend time with loved ones and friends.

- *Step #10* Give thanks for the power of intuition.

In addition to taking these ten action steps, remember that each time you read this book your intuition will open to its next level of awareness.

GUIDELINES FOR YOUR OWN INTUITION CIRCLE MASTERMIND GROUP

For the successful development of your intuition it is important that no one person is the leader of your group. Focus on an intention of love, supporting each other's intuition development, and leave your inner critic at the door. You may gather on the phone or in person for your Intuition Development Circle as often as you like. You may have a group of two to twenty people. Ideally your group will have between four and ten participants, but do not exclude anyone who is willing to learn and contribute to your group.

Rotate responsibilities between the various members of the group so that each week someone different can keep track of time and run your meeting effectively. Your group needs to agree to a regular schedule. For example, commit to meet every Wednesday from 5:00–6:00 P.M. If you commit to a schedule that you are struggling to keep, this will defeat the purpose of intuition development. Create balance. Review your commitments and adapt the meeting schedule if you need to by agreement with your group. Be sure that when you make your commitment to your circle you honor it.

I recommend you choose one chapter from *Unleash the Psychic in You* to discuss before the start of your meeting. I love Al-Anon's saying: "Take what you like and leave the rest." Remember that each person in your group is entitled to his or her own beliefs and opinions. Watch out for any hidden self-righteousness. Only share what is relevant to your intuition development. If someone doesn't ask for your advice, don't give it.

No bitching or talking behind people's backs. This will break your group apart fast.

Focus on the good progress you are making and avoid comparing yourself to the others in your group or taking on the mindset, "Our group is better than your group."

For additional information on how to set up and maintain your Intuition Circle Mastermind Group, and any feedback you'd like to share, please email: **info@AmericasIntuitionCoach.com**.

COOL INTUITION RESOURCES

Websites

www.AmericasIntuitionCoach.com

www.IntuitionSecrets.com

www.UnleashThePsychicInYou.com

www.JoannaGarzilli.com

www.IntuitionDevelopmentSystem.com

Confessions of a Psychic Weekly FREE Online Newsletter
(valued at $197)

For years I struggled with the need to be perfect. At the time I thought, "How can I help others if I'm not perfect?" In my popular weekly ezine, I confess all because many of my clients thought they had to have special abilities to be intuitive. Good news, all the answers you need are accessible within you. Each week I reveal confessions, tips, tools, and techniques to build confidence in your intuition so you can trust your own choices. You can make consistently successful decisions!

Intuition Secrets FREE Tuesday Teleseminars
(valued at $500)

In these FREE sixty-minute calls, learn firsthand the Seven Intuition Secrets that have made me America's Intuition Coach™ and how you can apply them to your own life. You don't want to miss this introductory call. Practicing just one of these intuition secrets will awaken your intuition now. To sign up for this informative call go to: **www.IntuitionSecrets.com/teleseminar**.

America's Intuition Coach™ Blog

Interested in having access to the latest tips and tools on intuition development? Look out for new information hot off the press! You can also write back to me on my blog: **www.AmericasIntuitionCoach.com**. I'd love to hear how you are progressing in your personal process of intuition development.

Intuition Development Home Study System™: How to Tune in and Trust Your Intuition and Apply the Seven Secrets to Successful Decision Making

If you are excited to take the next step in your intuition development and are ready to take full responsibility for your decision-making, then you will love the Intuition Development Home Study System™. It is packed with intuition development secrets and how-to techniques for use in your daily life that will support you in making successful decisions with ease and grace. Visit: **www.IntuitionDevelopmentSystem.com**.

Intuition Development Private Gold Circle

Limited availability. By application only. To receive an application, please email: **www.AmericasIntuitionCoach.com/ GoldCircle**

My "Intuition Secrets" Private Coaching Program

Limited availability. By application only. Learn how to make FAST, successful decisions and to overcome fear and self-doubt in order to double your income within six months and get all your needs met in every relationship!

Why do some people procrastinate when they know they need to make important decisions? As a result of past mistakes, they're scared that they're going to make a wrong choice and they're carrying unconscious shame and feelings of low self-esteem. Other people are waiting ready for opportunity to land in their laps while fearful people are still waiting, frustrated and depressed, as opportunity passes them by.

After fifteen years of successfully guiding hundreds of people one-on-one, I've developed decision-making techniques based on intuition that will move you beyond your financial blockages, relationship breakdowns, and lack of fulfillment in experiencing a purposeful career and life.

Intuition Secrets Coaching guides you step by step through powerful intuition development techniques and decision-making strategies that I have used to quadruple my income, marry my soul mate, and live my life purpose. It will help you to trust your intuition and never doubt your choices again.

I ONLY have space for a few one-on-one private clients, people who are serious about getting results and ready to accelerate success in their lives. If that sounds like you, to receive an application, please email: **info@AmericasIntuitionCoach.com.**

ABOUT THE AUTHOR

Using the same intuition secrets she teaches, Joanna Garzilli, America's Intuition Coach™, went from a failed relationship, being $100,000 debt, and suffering low self-esteem to being happily married, earning an income of $1,000+ per hour, and living her life purpose as a TV personality, author, and motivational speaker who helps people around the world to tune in and trust their intuition. Joanna has shared her wisdom on television with hundreds of thousands of people, teaching them how to increase their awareness and create the life they want to live within six months. Her clients include visionary entrepreneurs, entertainment professionals, including celebrity actors.

Joanna is the founder of **www.AmericasIntuitionCoach. com** and author of *Unleash the Psychic in You*, the most revealing book on the sixth sense of our time. Her book addresses how to overcome past feelings of failure and give yourself permission to step onto the path of your life purpose by trusting your intuition to make fast, successful decisions. Joanna is also the celebrated creator of the *Intuition Development Home Study System™, How to Tune-in and Trust Your Intuition and Apply the Seven Secrets to Successful Decision-Making.*

Joanna is respected for her ability and passion to help visionary entrepreneurs overcome their blind spots. She takes students to the next level of awareness with simple sensory techniques and visualization strategies that work fast by keeping them focused and on track. Joanna's motto for making the best and most empowering choice is: "Tune in. Trust it." She has a unique ability to get people to trust their intuition. Even if they've made mistakes and procrastinated, they now learn to make fast, confident decisions and experience a successful outcome every time.

You may contact Joanna Garzilli:

By Mail:

212 26th St, Suite 144

Santa Monica, CA 90402

By Phone:

1-877-822-5142 (toll free)

1-310-985-5163 (calling from outside the U.S.)

By Email:

info@AmericasIntuitionCoach.com

Via Website:

www.AmericasIntuitionCoach.com